Perspectives

Readings on American History in the 20th Century

Daniel J. Boorstin

Brooks Mather Kelley

Editors

with

Ruth Frankel Boorstin and Suzanne Grey Kelley

Prentice Hall

Needham, Massachusetts & Englewood Cliffs, New Jersey

CREDITS:

Editorial: David Lippman, Marie E. Norris
Design: Samuel S. Wallace
Photo Research: Russell Lappa
Production: Richard Ingram
Electronic Page Makeup: Peter Brooks
Marketing: Jeffrey M. Ikler, David R. Zarowin
Pre-press Production: Roger Powers
Manufacturing: Bill Wood

ISBN 0-13-387788-4

Printed in the United States of America

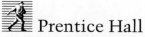 Prentice Hall

A Division of Simon & Schuster ● *Englewood Cliffs, New Jersey*

Table of Contents

FDR and the Legacy of the New Deal

The Decision to Drop the Atomic Bomb

Is the President Imperial?

The Impact of the Civil Rights Movement

Why Were We in Vietnam?

The Struggle for Women's Rights

The New Immigrants

After the Cold War—What Next?

To the Reader

This book gives you some perspectives on recent American history. It adds to your textbook and your understanding by showing different ways of looking at the facts in the story. And it focuses on movements and events so recent that new facts are still appearing about them. We go on trying to make up our minds about what these facts mean.

There are no subjects in American history—from the earliest colonial times to the present—on which the last word has been written. And though it may seem strange, the most recent events are often those that puzzle us the most and on which there is the widest disagreement. The essays printed here surely do not give the last word. But they offer perspectives that make the study of our recent history especially intriguing.

This volume is not intended to displace your textbook, but to supplement it. The following pages help us see how complex are all historical events and how many different ways there are of looking at them. From the history of the United States since World War I, we have selected ten subjects for the units that follow. These are especially interesting for study in greater depth. Here we offer the authors' varied views—perspectives—on the topic. The word "perspective" comes from Latin and means to see more clearly and in depth. We hope these writers will help you see these events in ways you might never have thought of. And we learn how the writers' own beliefs have shaped the meaning they find in the "facts." These beliefs sometimes help them decide what really is a fact.

Our authors touch many subjects, from politics and social history to the Constitution, and include military, diplomatic, and business history. Some topics like the role of the United States in the war in Vietnam are still matters of bitter disagreement. All these topics will remain open for discussion and will be debated by future historians. Some, like advertising and music, may seem less controversial, but they touch our everyday lives and help us understand ourselves.

We have prefaced each topic with an essay to help you weigh the significance of the subject. A few words before and after the essays identify the authors and their points of view, and tell where we found these observations. And we mention later events of special interest. As you read these "Perspectives," decide what the author is aiming at, compare the writer's ideas with those of others on the same subject, and then form your own opinion.

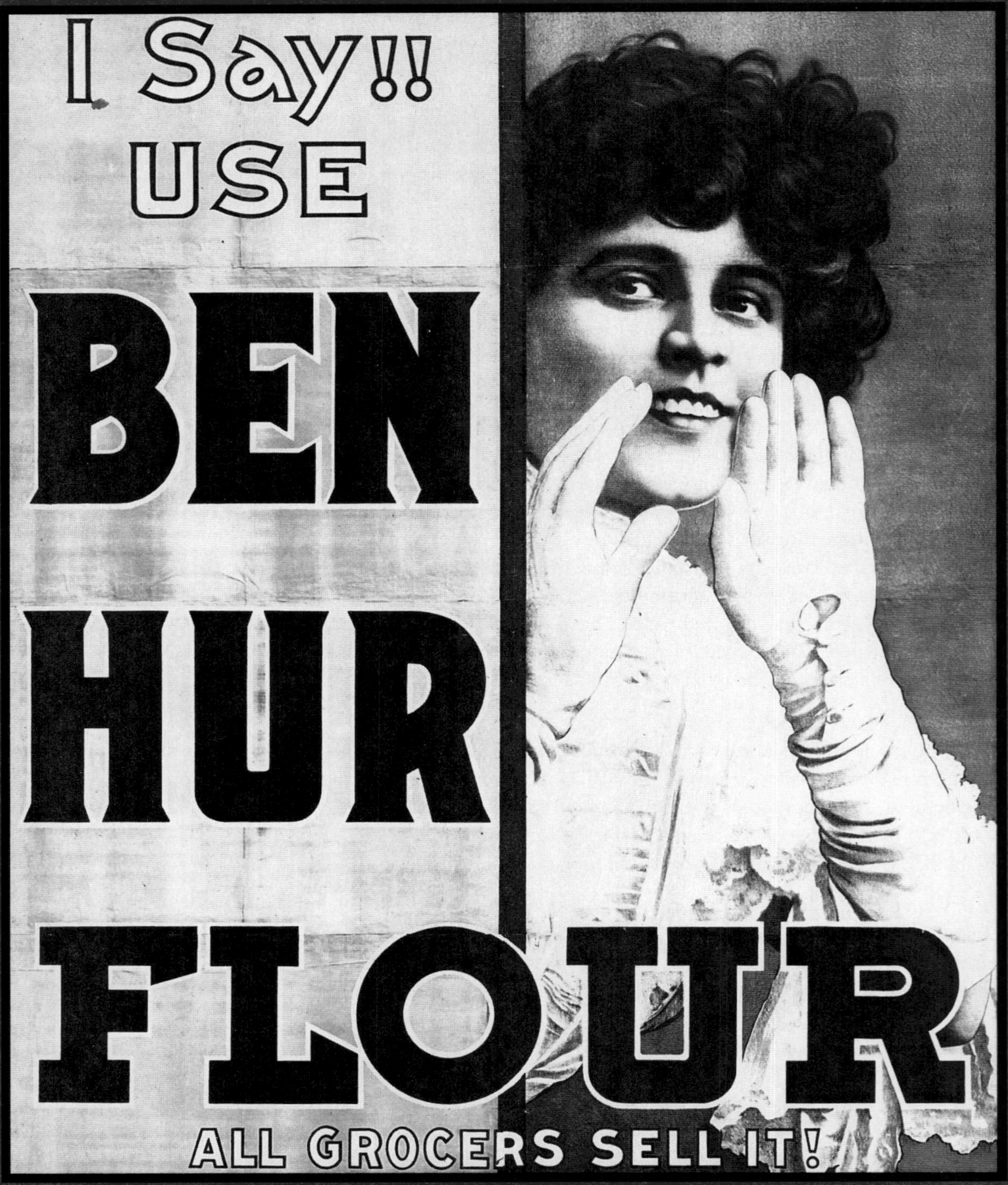
I Say!!
USE
BEN
HUR
FLOUR
ALL GROCERS SELL IT!

Perspectives on

ADVERTISING AND MASS CONSUMPTION

Advertising has been present ever since one human being wanted to sell something to another. Those first advertisements were oral: a statement that one wanted to buy or sell, or perhaps a crier walking through the streets hawking his wares. But written advertisements, too, have been around for a long time. One, an offer of a reward for a missing slave, some 3000 years old, was found in the ruins of Thebes. And in the Roman Empire professional poster painters put advertisements on the walls of buildings. Many of these have been discovered in the ruins of Pompeii.

It was not until the invention of movable type by Johann Gutenberg around 1450 that advertising moved into the "modern" age. Printing with movable type made it possible to get away from simple announcements (although these continue to this day) to a more compelling message—at first usually published in newspapers, but also in books, pamphlets, broadsheets, and handbills.

Fashions may change over the years, but in advertising the basic message always remains the same.

1

Early Advertising in America

America was born of advertising. One of the earliest and most persuasive advertisements for the new lands was Richard Hakluyt's *Voyages*, first published in 1582. Historian Samuel Eliot Morison said of this classic work, "His *Voyages*, in their several editions, have well been called the prose epic of the English nation. Not only was English literature enriched with hundreds of pithy sea narratives; they accomplished their author's purpose of firing his countrymen to worthy deeds overseas." Others, too, wrote books and pamphlets, and posted notices hoping to entice English men and women to leave hearth and home for the American wilderness. These advertisements for America painted a glowing picture of the New World. "The Healthfulness of the Air," said one advertisement for Carolina in 1666, "the Fertility of the Earth and Waters; and the great Pleasure and Profit will accrue to those that shall go thither to enjoy the same."

In the colonies most advertising was notices in the newspapers—like the one by Paul Revere in 1770 offering to make false teeth, which were not only ornamental but "of real use in Speaking and Eating." The early newspaper ads often ran unchanged for many months. But the creative editor James Gordon Bennett wanted his *New York Herald* to have "news" on every page—including the ads. So he barred the old standing advertisements, first saying in 1847 that an ad had to be changed every two weeks and then insisting that they be changed every day. Bennett's son realized that even the process of gathering the news could be news and good advertising for his newspaper as well. He proved this when he sent reporter Henry Stanley in 1871 to look for the missing Scottish missionary David Livingston in the heart of Africa, and made news while increasing the circulation of his paper.

Advertisements before the Civil War were generally directed at a local audience reached through handbills, posters, and signboards, along with brief notices in newspapers. But in the years between the Civil War and World War I, American life was transformed and advertising with it.

When the railways sent products to customers scattered across the country, national advertising and national brands developed. Without this new transportation network, Montgomery Ward and Sears, Roebuck would have been unable to deliver the products they showed in their catalogs. Americans, who before had made most things for themselves, met their needs with factory-made products from Ward and Sears. Or they bought from their neighborhood store items they saw advertised in the many inexpensive magazines and newspapers of the day.

Advertising and Mass Consumption in Modern America

After World War I American advertising boomed. The major carriers were the familiar newspapers, magazines, and billboards, assisted by direct mail. But the fastest growing vehicle of advertising was the radio, the new gadget that spread across America during the 1920s (see pp. 30-32). On the eve of World War I, total American expenditures on advertising ran about $1 billion per year. By 1929 advertising costs had zoomed to $3.4 billion a year and the nation had entered the age of mass consumption.

After World War II, television became an important new way for advertisers to reach prospective customers. In 1948 there were only 200,000 TV sets in all the United States, but twenty years later 95 percent of all American homes had at least one TV set. At the same time, advertising through radio, newspapers, magazines, billboards, and direct mail continued to reach consumers in vast numbers. By 1990 the top 100 national advertisers were spending all together more than $30 billion dollars per year on advertising. The single biggest advertiser, Philip Morris, spent more than $2 billion.

Advertising can exist without mass consumption. In the Soviet Union and other totalitarian countries, governments use ads to praise the state, the Communist party, and the dictators in power. But when goods are scarce as they are in those countries, there is no point in advertising individual products, since people wait in line and scramble anyway for whatever appears on the store shelves. In a free enterprise country like ours, mass consumption could scarcely exist without advertising. In the midst of abundance, the consumer turns to the advertiser for guidance. What's new? Where can I find it? Why is it better than a competing product? What does it cost? These messages, broadcast in a variety of ways, help both the manufacturer and the consumer.

In the readings below, we have chosen excerpts that reveal some of the many ways of looking at advertising and mass consumption in our land of plenty.

Madison Avenue in New York City is home to many ad agencies. To many people it is the symbol of the advertising world.

INTRODUCTION   In *The Great Bull Market: Wall Street in the 1920s*, historian Robert Sobel described the factors that fed the stock market boom of the 1920s. What elements, according to Sobel, created the consumerism of the decade?

Perspective 1

An Age of Innovation and Growth

*by **Robert Sobel***

More important than the foreign markets…[to American business] was the growth in America of what came to be called "consumerism." Before the [first world] war, credit for consumers' goods was granted, but not exploited. For the most part, the would-be purchaser of an appliance or home improvement believed he would need cash before entering a store. One of the reasons Henry Ford struggled to bring down the price of his Model "T" was to enable millions who otherwise could not afford an automobile to purchase one. But Ford was unwilling to base his sales campaign on credit; although dealers would sell on time, they were discouraged from doing so by the factory.

Similarly, advertising was still in its infancy in 1914. Department stores, national branded goods, and some local products took out advertisements in newspapers, and billboards were common sights, but most appeals were crude, unimaginative, sober, and ill conceived. What was needed at this time was a concerted campaign, deployed through the proper media, and tied to credit purchases. All three came together in the early twenties.

The possibilities of consumerism were obvious to many businessmen before the war. The nation was in a recession in 1913, with attendant unemployment and closed factories. Millions of Americans were without many of the basic necessities of life, not to mention what at the time seemed luxuries, such as indoor plumbing and electrification. It was clear, even then, that the nation's factories were capable of turning out goods that would raise the living standard dramatically, but that potential consumers lacked the wherewithal to purchase these goods. As late as 1920 there were only thirteen bathtubs and six telephones for every hundred people in the nation's cities, and the figures were lower for the farm population. Although one family in three had an automobile, less than one in 10,000 owned a radio. One out of every ten city dwellings was electrified; almost no farms had electricity. Should wires be brought to these homes, their owners would become customers for the great variety of appliances then being offered. If radios and indoor plumbing could be purchased with low initial payments, then millions might avail themselves of these "innovations."

With the return of prosperity and the rapid expansion of the economy following the postwar depression, many firms began to mount large-scale advertising campaigns tied to credit buying. Bruce Barton, a pioneer of modern advertising and one of the prophets of the period, intuitively recognized that this was the key to increased sales, higher profits, and a better standard of living. In 1924 he attempted to give selling a moral flavor as well. In that year he reflected on his lack of interest as a youth in the Bible.

Automobiles opened up new vistas to Americans. This family has traveled over the rough roads of the time in its Model T Ford for a picnic in the country.

This was because he was repelled by the image of Jesus most writers offered. But then, according to Barton, he reread the book and realized that Jesus was not a weakling, a dreamer, or a person interested only in other-worldly affairs. Instead, He was a man who "picked up twelve men from the bottom ranks of business and forged them into an organization that conquered the world."

> Some day...someone will write a book about Jesus. Every business man will read it and send it to his partners and his salesmen. For it will tell the story of the founder of modern business.

Barton wrote the book himself, *The Man Nobody Knows*, and it became the bestselling work of the year. Business was moral, selling was akin to prayer, and God meant us to enjoy ourselves on Earth, was his message. *The Man Nobody Knows* did not mould the decade's atmosphere, but did reflect the changes Barton and his followers were bringing to the marketplace. Three years later Wesley C. Mitchell, one of the nation's leading economists, put matters in a more scholarly context.

5

Yet with all their puzzles, consumers are in a strong market position. Their formal freedom to spend their money incomes as they like, combined with their massive inertia, keeps producers under pressure to solicit customers, to teach the public to want more goods and new goods. This task of stimulating demand is never done; for the march of technological improvement is ever increasing our capacity to produce, and before we have learned to distribute and to use what has just been added to our output, new advances have been scored. Hence the chronic complaint of businessmen that our industries are "over built."

What both men were saying, in effect, was that the new era of American capitalism had seen an end in many fields of competition in prices and variety of products; it was one in which firms and products would compete on the basis of advertisements, credit, and services. Mitchell's businessmen were concerned about rapid technological change, but this was not their major problem. Nor were industries "over built" in 1927. Instead the factories, stimulated by the growth of consumerism earlier in the decade, were on the verge of overproducing after a generation of underproducing.

Consumerism was stoked by large infusions of advertising capital. Figures on these expenses were not calculated before the war, but estimates vary between $350 million and $400 million. In contrast, $1.5 billion was spent on advertising in 1927. The largest amount—$690 million—went to newspapers. Another $210 million was spent on magazines, and $75 million on billboards. Only $7 million was spent for radio advertisements that year, but this was the fastest growing segment of the industry. Direct mailings and announcements accounted for some $400 million, with the rest distributed to trade jour-

Ford announced with pride its new 1909 five-passenger touring car, which it claimed was as good as any car selling for several hundred dollars more.

nals, streetcar signs, and other media. And still the field expanded. By 1929, more than $1.8 billion was being spent on advertising.

Consumer goods which might be purchased on time accounted for the bulk of the new advertisements. For example, magazine ads for radios rose from less than $80,000 in 1922 to $3.4 million in 1927. There were few advertisements for electric refrigerators in 1922; by 1927 more than $1.5 million was spent to advertise them. Automobiles, which accounted for less than 10 per cent of newspaper ads in 1922, rose to 19.3 per cent in 1927. And other consumer durables were not far behind.

AFTERWORD   The weakness of the consumerism of the 1920s was that while workers were producing more than ever before, their wages, even though rising, did not keep pace with the increase in production. The difference, for a while, was made up by buying "on time." But when consumers used up all their credit, they had to stop buying. Then sales fell. This was a serious flaw in the prosperity of the 1920s which helped worsen the Great Depression of the 1930s when it came.

This selection is reprinted from THE GREAT BULL MARKET, Wall Street in the 1920s, by Robert Sobel with the permission of W.W. Norton & Company, Inc. Copyright © 1968 by W.W. Norton & Company, Inc.

ADVERTISING AND MASS CONSUMPTION

INTRODUCTION   Charles Goodrum was formerly with the
Library of Congress, and his co-author Helen Dalrymple is on the staff of
the Library. In the excerpt below from their volume *Advertising in America:
The First Two Hundred Years*, they point out some of the difficulties of persuading people to buy frozen food once it was invented. The manufacturers of all new products, from automobiles to computers, have faced similar problems of swaying people to buy something they did not know they
needed. What were some of the obstacles frozen food had to overcome?
How did advertising help?

Perspective 2

The Educator of New Technology

*by **Charles Goodrum** and **Helen Dalrymple***

There is general agreement that there are few things advertising does as well as introducing new inventions to the community. From the days of the sewing machine and the reaper to the hand-held calculator and ballpoint pen, it has done its job honestly and, even more surprisingly, with an astonishing restraint. In view of the typical ad writer's oversell, you will find the "first ads for…" remarkably temperate—almost understated….

The ads provoke another…thought. In almost every case, what they are selling is going to cost more than what the invention would replace. The new product thus must be added on to current expenses. Where does the money come from to pay for all these things? We find the answer in two places.

First, the money for the purchase itself usually came through some form of installment payments, which was an idea that had begun as far back as the early sewing machines in the 1850s. (…[A]n early Singer [sewing machine] cost $125 when the average annual family income of the time was barely $500.) And then, sec-ond, the installments were paid off through the ever-rising standard of living of the American family. One of the endless arguments among economists is stirred up by this progression. You can either perceive this stream of new things that we "really must have" as driving us on to greater productivity, higher wages, and a more sat-isfying life-style; or you can see it as locking the average man into hopeless, despairing, never-resolved debt, and a perpetual sense of failure.

…A new product demands education in many forms. A classic example was the introduction of frozen foods. General Foods

bought Clarence Birdseye's rights and patents in 1929. It spent several years testing to find out which foods were most appropriate to the new idea; which could actually be frozen, which still tasted like fresh when they were prepared and served. General Foods next went to the Young & Rubicam ad agency to work up how to announce the innovation and how to explain how to use it. Once the campaign was laid out, the company and the agency selected Springfield, Massachusetts, as a test site and moved in.

The company offered freezer chests to grocery stores to hold the new product, and offered the product on consignment to twenty grocers to sell it. The agency got the local papers to run stories about the potential revolution in food habits, and distributed 16mm films to local service clubs for "how-to" programs. For the two-month test period, it took out newspaper ads pushing different frozen products: oysters, spring lamb, beef pot roast, and the expected series of vegetables. James Playsted Wood, who was

There were many difficulties in getting the new product of frozen food from the factory to the consumer, not least the need for grocers to have freezers.

9

involved in the initial presentation, recalls that there were problems. The freezer chests had to be upgraded, and the housewives stubbornly refused to "thaw before using," which caused much frustration on all sides. Preparation time thus exceeded that for simply opening a can, and the requirements for seasoning had to be slowly learned. Ultimately, however, the reduced waste, the time saved in preparation, and the year-round variety and availability of the foods won out, and almost ten years after the project started, the product became an accepted part of the family diet. Throughout the campaign, the advertising agency not only played a major role in the explanation and education aspects, but an equally important one in testing, probing, and experimenting to determine where the resistance to the innovation lay and what could be done about it. The pattern of presentation was finally repeated in communities all around the country.

When Birdseye frozen foods, then called "frosted foods," were introduced in Springfield, Massachusetts, in 1939, the wonders of the new product had to be explained.

AFTERWORD   Before frozen foods could succeed in the marketplace, stores had to have special freezers to hold and display the product, homes had to have freezer compartments in their refrigerators, and housewives had to learn how to cook the various products. But, aided by advertising, within a decade frozen foods had become a multibillion-dollar business with many companies competing for the consumers' money.

INTRODUCTION   While some observers, like Goodrum and Dalrymple in the previous selection, found advertising useful, especially for the introduction of new products, others saw its perils. Writer Ron Goulart, in the excerpt that follows from his 1969 book *The Assault on Childhood*, objects to its influence. What did he point to as the most dangerous effect of advertising on children? What do both critics and defenders agree on about the aims of advertising directed at children?

Perspective 3

The Assault on Childhood

*by **Ron Goulart***

Many of the children in America will never grow up. The odds are mounting, the obstacles and hazards increasing. Most of our kids are under attack, and the attack has both physical and psychological effects. Physically, of course, most of them will probably survive. They all stand, however, in danger of never growing up inside, of being trapped for the length of their lives in an endless childhood or a false adulthood. Childhood should be a journey, and one of its joys is being able to travel through it to the next stage. How hard and how fulfilling this journey is depends chiefly on the child and the parent. Increasingly, though, outsiders are intruding and setting up blocks to progress.

These outsiders [are] the people to whom kids are big business....

Since there has been a United States, there has been a kid market here. The abusing and exploiting of children has a venerable history, though there has never before been anything like today's situation. The Second World War, something no member of the youth market remembers, was the basic cause. The war reshaped family patterns, allowing for a youth culture to grow and spread. It brought a new affluence.

The confrontation of kids and advertisers was also encouraged by the rise of television. Advertisers found the teenagers first, then children from 12 on down. In 1939 only $300,000 was spent on advertising to young people on network radio. In less than twenty years, the budget for youth advertising, on television, rose to over 100 million dollars.

Our kids today represent yearly gross sales that have been estimated as high as 50 billion dollars. There are several billion more to be made from adult sales influenced by child pressure. About two and a half billion of the annual take goes to the toy tycoons....

Another big share of the youth market profits goes to the soft drink makers. They sell almost three and a half billion dollars worth

11

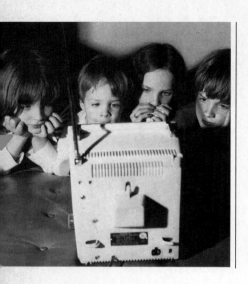

Children were transfixed by television and even found the advertisements fascinating.

of flavored water a year, much of it to kids. Coca-Cola does 40 percent of all this business, trailed by Pepsi-Cola and Royal Crown. Candy costs us a billion and a half dollars. Children spend 25 million dollars just on bubble gum. Of children, a bubble gum vice president says, "That's who we're after every day, every month, all the time." The breakfast food industry persuades kids to consume 650 million dollars' worth of dry cereal annually. To do this, Kellogg, General Mills, Quaker Oats, General Foods, and Ralston spend 100 million dollars on advertising. "The cereal companies often spend more to promote," reports Forbes, the business magazine, "than to produce what they sell." Kellogg alone puts out something like 15 million dollars on network television advertising, putting them up in the top twenty of television advertisers and giving them considerable control over what kind of programs kids will see.... [1]

Both critics and defenders of the consumer conditioning of children seem to agree on its aims. David Riesman, as long ago as 1950, observed in The Lonely Crowd that the long-range object of the mass media assault on children was to build up in the child "habits of consumption he will employ as an adult." In the early 1960's, social anthropologist Jules Henry pointed out that all cultures train children "for the roles they will fill as adults." In our society, "the central aims of our culture are to sell goods,...create consumers,...educate children to buy."

AFTERWORD   How much of the effect of advertising on children is due to the reluctance of parents to say no to buying a new toy or breakfast food that has been advertised on TV? Advertisements are only efforts to persuade. A democratic society must depend on the ability of citizens to resist politicians and advertisers who try to mislead them. But TV provides a new and dangerously vivid form of persuasion.

---

[1] Spending today is much greater. In 1988, Kellogg spent $683 million. *Eds.*

INTRODUCTION   Max Lerner is a journalist and teacher who has written on a broad range of subjects. The excerpt below is from his wide-ranging book, *America as a Civilization: Life and Thought in the United States Today* (1957–1987). What does Lerner believe are some of the effects on Americans of living in "a wilderness of commodities"? Does he agree with those who think that Americans are not materialists?

Perspective 4

The Wilderness of Commodities

by Max Lerner

T he world of the consumer which results from American work and technology is one of profusion and variety. The consumer lives in a wilderness of commodities whose impact on the minds of Americans themselves, as on that of the world, is one of richness. American living standards are the boast of politicians and editorial writers and the target of sermons, and during the Cold War they were a main reliance in American psychological warfare against Communist systems. "No ordinary Russian," [advertising pioneer] Bruce Barton told a convention of salesmen, "ever suspected such a wealth of wonderful and desirable objects exists anywhere in the world as the Sears, Roebuck catalogue presents." On a more academic level [social scientist] David Riesman ironically told (in "The Nylon War") how the hold of the Russian rulers was broken by a military campaign of bombarding them with millions of pairs of nylon stockings and other items from the American cornucopia. For the ordinary American the belief in the idea of progress is reinforced by the visible sign of his rising living standards. Adapting a phrase of [historian Arnold] Toynbee's, one might call this the "idolization of ephemeral enjoyments." The popular literature and culture celebrate not technology or even business and the making of money but the grandeurs and miseries of a consumer's civilization. America seems strikingly to illustrate [sociologist Pitirim] Sorokin's category of the "sensate culture."

This has led to an indictment of Americans as "materialists," which has generally been accepted by both Americans and foreigners, by the intellectuals as well as the preachers. Recently some of the intellectuals have begun to question the indictment. "The virtue of American civilization," [writer] Mary McCarthy has ventured, "is that it is unmaterialistic. It is true that America produces and consumes more cars, more soap and bathtubs, than any other nation, but we live *among* these objects rather than *by* them...."

13

Consumers in the United States are faced with a confusing array of products.

The comfortable, the convenient, the clean, the polished and glittering, the ingenious, the novel, the extra bit of service: these form some of the ingredients of American "materialism." And the most marked ingredient of all, containing and encompassing all the rest, is the overwhelming measure of American consumer abundance.

It is as wide of the mark to deride this as "a Coca-Cola civilization" as it is to use the standard N.A.M. [National Association of Manufacturers] argument that this plenitude of products and gadgets is proof of America's having found the key to a good life. Actually there is a grotesque disproportion about the national values which is revealed by the direction of American spending. More is spent on cosmetics, tobacco, liquor, than on public education. The health services are relatively starved, the serious arts are sometimes neglected. And for one American family out of four or five, life is still a rat race of worry, work, and scrimping.

It remains true, however, that there are more good things available to a higher proportion of Americans than in any other society. This is not a matter of piglike, sensuous reveling in material things. The long-established image of America as a kind of golden sty is a

14

stereotype with more envy and ignorance than truth. The vast array of available commodities has become an American way of living, but it does not follow that Americans are more likely than others to confuse living standards with life values, or mistake good things for the good life. Many Americans—like many other human beings—do live *by* things as well as *among* them. But many others know that, like the machine, the shopwindow crowded with glittering items carries no ethic with it. It does not become an end in itself except for the impoverished of spirit, who are to be found in any civilization. What is true in America is that they find it easier to disguise their impoverished spirit behind the gaudy raiments of a consumer's plenty.

AFTERWORD   The selection of products from all over the world that Americans can buy has increased in every decade since World War II, and Americans continue to love to be attracted by new gadgets as they appear. The criticism of their priorities, as reflected in their spending habits, remains today much like what Lerner described.

INTRODUCTION   Historian Daniel J. Boorstin is the Librarian of Congress Emeritus and co-editor of this book. He has often written about advertising and its role in American life. The selection below is from a 1980 speech to members of the advertising industry. What does he mean when he refers to advertising as "good news"? How has advertising, according to Boorstin, been integrated into our lives?

Perspective 5

The Good News of Advertising

by Daniel J. Boorstin

The United States is perhaps the first nation in history in whose founding advertising played a crucial role. The founders of Massachusetts Bay colony and Virginia and of most of the other colonies, including especially Georgia, used advertising to attract both investors and settlers.

The growth of the British colonies in America, then, is one of the first success stories in modern advertising. This gives us a clue to the significance of advertising in American life and also to two features on which I want to focus our attention briefly.

First, advertising began as good news. If advertising is the rhetoric of democracy, it has also carried the gospel of American ways of life.

Voice of Choice

The Declaration of Independence is one of the first and most successful examples of institutional advertising in America, the institution, of course, being a new nation. Later, with the rise of the periodical press and then the daily press, advertising became product advertising. We must be wary of those who insist on the sharp distinction between product advertising and other forms....

The first characteristic then, historically, is that advertising began as good news. The second is that advertising has been a symbol of voluntariness. It is an educational device to provide opportunities for freedom of choice. Those who advertised the colonies said, *choose* America. Advertising obviously is futile and superfluous when there is no opportunity for choice, for choice of product or choice of attitudes. The flourishing of advertising then is a clue to the increasing opportunities for choice.

When my wife Ruth and I were recently and briefly in the Soviet Union as guests of the Minister of Culture, we did occasionally watch television. And when we came back and turned on our American television sets, instead of feeling the familiar irritation at the interruption of commercials...we bought a little box of tapers and we lit a taper any time a commercial appeared, since the commercial was an icon of freedom...a sign that we had the opportunity to choose.

The question then, today and in the coming decades is, can advertising fulfill these two historic roles? Can advertising still be both a bringer of good news and a symbol of voluntariness? In our age of broadcasting can it continue to be so?

...[T]he role of advertising as an American institution embedded in American life is very recent, extremely recent. And it's symbolized in certain ways, for example in the two-way movement between advertising persons, activities, institutions and products of the so-called fine arts.

"Pop artists" painted pictures of products from everyday life. Andy Warhol created "Campbell Soup Can With Peeling Label" in 1962.

New Roles To Fill

The rise of pop art in the 1950s and '60s and '70s, the works of Andy Warhol, Roy Lichtenstein and Claes Oldenburg all have been signs that advertising has become not merely a major American institution but has become embedded in the very texture of our fine arts. The images of advertising have recently taken on a wide esthetic significance.

...[I]n the June 23, 1980, issue of *The New Yorker* [there was] an interesting advertisement by Hasselblad. The advertisement reads, "Conversation piece. This full size replica of the world famous Hasselblad 500 CM is hand-crafted of Swedish crystal—a fitting tribute to the camera that went to the moon. Each piece is numbered and signed by the artist, and will undoubtedly become a collector's item. The Hasselblad Swedish crystal camera, at $265, is available at better camera stores that carry the real thing: Hasselblad cameras."

17

Conversation piece

This full size replica of the world famous Hasselblad 500 C/M is hand-crafted of Swedish crystal—a fitting tribute to the camera that went to the moon.

Each piece is numbered and signed by the artist, and will undoubtedly become a collector's item.

The Hasselblad Swedish crystal camera, at $265, is available at better camera stores that carry the real thing: Hasselblad cameras.

If you give us your name and address, we will mail one of our beautiful folders.

HASSELBLAD

Victor Hasselblad Inc. ☐ 10 Madison Road ☐ Fairfield, N.J. 07006

Masterpiece

The Hasselblad 500 C/M is more than a camera—it's a work of art. An outstanding example of purity of design and uncompromising quality. Hasselblad was the camera chosen by NASA to go the the moon.

It's been chosen by museums to exemplify the high degree of artistry that technology can reach.

It's the choice of serious photographers the world over.

See the Hasselblad 500 C/M—the world's most respected camera—at fine photo stores, or write for a luxurious folder to:

HASSELBLAD

Victor Hasselblad Inc. ☐ 10 Madison Road ☐ Fairfield, N.J. 07006

Hasselblad called the artistic copy of its own camera "a conversation piece," but the actual machine-made camera they considered a "masterpiece."

This use of a "hand-crafted" image of the machine-made product as an advertisement, and the willingness of people to pay a substantial price for an image of the product, signal a new relationship of advertising to American life and to the arts in America. Advertising will really have come into its own when the art work—this Swedish crystal image of the Hasselblad—this modern Wooden Indian—is more costly than the camera itself!

This two-way movement—from the arts into the world—and vice versa—plainly shows how fully advertising has been integrated into our life. On radio and on the television screen, dramatic techniques also have taken on a new significance for advertising.

Borrowed Techniques

Television advertising now, of course, uses the techniques of the western, of the detective mystery and even, *mirabile dictu* [amazing to relate], of the soap serial itself. We have found a new way to document Oscar Wilde's profound witticism, that nature imitates art. Now our life imitates advertising. Some of us sit through the program so that we can watch the commercial. We use that handy little device (I have no doubt that it was promoted by the advertising industry) which makes it possible, without getting up from our seat, to turn off the sound until the commercial comes back on.

Of course there are also many suspenseful dramatic episodes every day in the advertising industry itself. These have become the subject of some of our most interesting and lively television programs on the great successes and melodramatic failures of national advertising campaigns—for Presidents or other products. And then there is the new love triangle—the account executive, the client, and the media.

The Picasso exhibit at the Museum of Modern Art in New York [in 1980] shows us how the greatest, most versatile artist of the century can (even after his death) create a promotional project for IBM and other sponsors. Art has become advertising, advertising has become art.

Encyclopedias Notice It

Another clue to the wider, subtler role of advertising in our life is found in the Encyclopedia Britannica. The fourteenth edition of the Encyclopedia, published in 1956, has a considerable article on advertising. In fact that article is longer than the article in the later edition, under the same title. That 1956 article defines advertising in the first sentence: "Advertising is the process of disseminating information for commercial purposes." The latest edition of the Britannica (copyright 1980), describes the subject of its article as follows: "Advertising is a form of communication intended to promote the sale of a product or service, to influence public opinion, to gain political support, to advance a particular cause, or to elicit some other response desired by the advertiser." At long last our encyclopedia writers have begun to recognize the significance of this institution in American life.

But the academic profession in general is very slow to catch up with the realities of everyday experience. There are courses in advertising in business schools and in commercial colleges, but my colleagues the historians have not yet fully admitted advertising to their list of the significant topics of social history.

AFTERWORD   Advertising has been criticized for creating unnecessary wants. But as Boorstin makes clear, many of our most cherished and most indispensable modern devices were originally unnecessary. No one needed an automobile until after it was invented and roads were built for them. Then advertising brought the good news of the automobile and later helped us to choose between a bewildering variety of different models.

From "The Good News of Advertising" by Daniel J. Boorstin. Reprinted with permission from *Advertising Age*, November 13, 1980. Copyright, Crain Communications Inc., 1980.

Perspectives on

AMERICAN MUSIC IN THE JAZZ AGE

The 1920s have the distinction of two lively nicknames: the Roaring Twenties and the Jazz Age. And both names fit those years of loud fast rhythms. But like all nicknames they tell only part of the story.

In Search of Normalcy

It was a time of booming factories, when iceboxes were displaced by refrigerators, when horses were crowded off the roads by speeding automobiles, when radios came into American living rooms and kitchens, a time of fancy movie houses and brilliant movie stars. But it was also to be an age of disillusionment, rebellion, and escapism. After World War I people were tired of high-minded preachments like those of President Woodrow Wilson. His successor from a small Ohio town, Warren G. Harding, was a handsome man of few talents. In his inaugural address Harding called for no great crusades but wished only for a return to

Cab Calloway (right) and his orchestra were one of the popular musical groups that played in Chicago in the 1920s.

21

In both his books and his own life novelist F. Scott Fitzgerald revealed many of the excesses of the Jazz Age.

"normalcy." Americans were ready to insulate themselves from the evil world "out there." Harding himself tried to escape the cares of being President in poker games with his home-state buddies, the "Ohio Gang," who dominated his political decisions and brought scandal to the White House.

Disillusion with the results of World War I and yearning for "normalcy" stirred the anger of small-town America against "sinful" cities and bred fear of recent immigrants. The Ku Klux Klan thrived on hatred of blacks, Jews, Catholics, and all foreigners. The new immigration acts (p. 168) limited the number of newcomers and favored those who came from northern and western Europe. The trial of John T. Scopes in Tennessee for teaching evolution expressed the fear of science and the unwillingness to move into the modern era.

Many people in cities turned away from the traditions and morals of farming America. The journalist and critic H. L. Mencken poked fun at small-town Americans whom he called the "Booboisie" or "boobus Americanus," and he ridiculed the three-time presidential candidate William Jennings Bryan for his prosecution of Scopes for teaching evolution.

Mencken and others in the twenties freely criticized their fellow Americans. And the disillusionment of the intellectuals was best represented by T. S. Eliot, the poet from St. Louis who fled to England, portrayed a degraded and bleak modern world in his poem *The Waste Land*. The combination of disillusionment and the vigor to criticize produced a blossoming of American literature in the works of Theodore Dreiser, Ring Lardner, Sherwood Anderson, Sinclair Lewis, F. Scott Fitzgerald, Ernest Hemingway, and Eugene O'Neill.

Boom—and Bust

The Jazz Age, the Roaring Twenties, brought the optimism of thriving factories, burgeoning jazz, speakeasies and bootleggers, skinny flappers drinking liquor and smoking cigarettes, rebellious young people rejecting the beliefs of their elders. From this frantic activity came two booms— the wild speculation in Florida real estate and the rising stock market.

In one of the nation's largest and quickest migrations, Americans rushed to Florida in the mid-twenties to buy land in a sunny climate which could now be easily reached by the automobile. Reckless optimistic investors bought lots sight unseen that sometimes were under water, in resort cities that did not exist. But the Florida boom was blown away in the hurricane of 1926 which showed (as historian Frederick Lewis Allen observed) "what a soothing tropic wind could do when it got a running start from the West Indies."

Despite the Florida collapse, the stock market boomed. The continuing rise gave people who did not even own any stocks a false sense of prosperity. Everyone knew of someone who had "struck it rich" on the stock market. And then the Great Crash of 1929 brought a resounding end to all these dreams. In that year journalist Walter Lippmann wrote of the young people whose freewheeling behavior (along with the great bull market) still colors our view of the time:

> What most distinguishes the generation who have approached maturity since the debacle of idealism at the end of the War is not their rebellion against the religion and the moral code of their parents, but their disillusionment with their own rebellion. It is common for young men and women to rebel, but that they should rebel sadly and without faith in their own rebellion, that they should distrust the new freedom no less than the old certainties— that is something of a novelty.

The 1920s were many things to many people. Because of the new sounds that filled the air in those years and christened them the Jazz Age, we have chosen in this unit to concentrate on the music of the time. What was that music? Who made it? Who heard it? How did they dance to it, and what did it mean to them?

INTRODUCTION   Journalist Mark Sullivan's six-volume *Our Times* is a classic of American social history. In the selection below from the last volume of the series, *The Twenties*, Sullivan discusses some popular songs and how they expressed the era. Some others were "Makin' Whoopee," "Yes, We Have No Bananas," and the nonsense song "Horses," whose first verse read (and the other verses were similar), "Horses, Horses, Horses! Nutty over Horses, Horses, Horses! Goofy over Horses, Horses, Horses!"

Perspective 1

Tunes of the Twenties

by **Mark Sullivan**

"The history of a country is written in its popular songs; from time immemorial current events have found lyric expression through the people's self-appointed troubadours, and such vocal outbursts have often had a real significance in reflecting the spirit, the atmosphere, the customs, the manners, and morals of the day."— Sigmund Spaeth

Serious acceptance of the theory that "the history of a country is written in its popular songs" would lead to distortion of a sort not uncommon when history is made to conform to a formula, and facts ingeniously mobilized to support a theory. But, accepting popular songs as a facet of the times, we might say, without too much straining, that the decade of the 1920's had as its overture the serene and confident *Smiles* [There are smiles that make us happy, There are smiles that make us blue, There are smiles that steal away the teardrops, As the sunbeams steal away the dew....], that it rose to a fortissimo which might be expressed in a paean of exuberant affluence, *My God, How the Money Rolls In*, and that it ended, after the panic of 1929, with a crashing finale—"crashing" is in this connection an especially apt adjective—the universally familiar and uniquely appropriate song of indigence, *Brother, Can You Spare a Dime?*

Brother, Can You Spare a Dime? was a true "topical" song, had a direct and intended relation to the time. It was composed during the depression, was inspired by the depression, and reflected the depression mood. The song was an essential part of the depression years, as characteristic, and as familiar, as bank-closings, money-hoarding, and seedy-genteel men selling apples on street-corners. As music, or as verse, the song was not much. What mainly gave it

24

the vogue it had was the unique appropriateness of its title.

After a while the title cut itself loose from the song and acquired a standing of its own. The words "Brother, can you spare a dime?" became a saying, a comment, the equivalent of a shrug of the shoulders, serving for the depression years the same function that "c'est la guerre" had filled during the Great War. The words "Brother, can you spare a dime?" with the tone in which they were said, the union of appeal for help with resignation to adversity, made it the complete and adequate summary of the spirit of the day. Occasionally it was said with bitterness; but it conformed more closely to the American spirit on the more frequent occasions when it was spoken with humor, humor sustained under hard conditions.

For a song to express the boom-peak of the decade, we should be obliged to go back to an old ditty which during the Twenties experienced a revival and an adaptation. *My God, How the Money Rolls In,* sung with exuberant gusto, was an accurate expression of the late 1920's, but the original words had been written many years before:

When the plea, "Brother, Can You Spare a Dime?" was heard, it was clear the happy days of the Jazz Age were over.

> My sister she works in the laundry,
> My father he fiddles for gin,
> My mother she takes in washing,
> My God! how the money rolls in!

By changing the second line to

> My father sells bootlegger gin

or

> My father makes synthetic gin,

the Twenties gave to the song a timeliness which related it to the "easy money" phase of the decade, and also made it appropriate to another aspect of the period. The allusions to specifically described

25

sources of easy money provided humor to a generation just becoming familiar with outlawed—but not successfully exiled—substitutes for liquor. A good many Americans of 1920 and subsequent years never heard the word "synthetic" except as an adjective describing gin.

AFTERWORD   Sullivan pointed out elsewhere in his book that there was another side to the twenties. The one song that he thought broke through the veneer was the timeless "Ol' Man River" (1927). In it the River, the Mississippi, "jes keeps rollin' along," indifferent to all the hardships of the people living and working on its banks. The charismatic black actor and singer Paul Robeson sang it so movingly that the song practically became identified with him.

Talented actor and singer Paul Robeson was a strong advocate of black rights when that was still unusual. This photograph was taken in the 1930s.

INTRODUCTION   Social historian Russell Lynes, in his spright-
ly volume *The Lively Audience*, from which the selection below is taken,
describes how and where Americans heard jazz (or what they often mis-
takenly called jazz). He also notes how many members of the older generation disapproved of this new music. There was similar outrage in the
1950s when rock 'n' roll came along.

·——◦◦◦◦——·

Perspective 2

Blues, Boogie-woogie, Swing

by Russell Lynes

The number of Americans who heard jazz not on records but at first hand was very limited indeed. The real jazz was being performed in what to most good citizens were disreputable places—nightclubs, speakeasies, roadhouses, dance halls, and other "low dives" of one sort or another. The prosperous young, who cavorted in the Jazz Age and who were the despair of their shocked and anxious parents, drove, especially if they lived in the suburbs or the country, in their roadsters or touring cars to roadhouses—restaurants and speakeasies with small bands and napkin-size dance floors. Ostensibly one had to have a card to get in, but a self-assured look was usually enough to convince the man who peered through the peephole in the door.

In the more expensive roadhouses colored lights played on a revolving, many-faceted, mirrored ball above the dance floor and cast flickering patches, like an animated stained-glass window, on the walls and on the customers who sat at their little tables, some-times with their liquor in teacups, and on those who jostled each other on the dance floor. (It was a primitive version of what in the 1960s became "light shows," usually with strobe lights....) In most such places the music was a sweetened and diluted version of jazz, a far cry from [Jelly Roll] Morton's Red Hot Peppers or [Louis] Armstrong's Hot Seven. The tunes were from musical comedies and Broadway "revues"—the *Ziegfeld Follies* or *George White's Scandals*, or *The Garrick Gaieties*. It was the era of tunes like "Tea for Two," "Indian Love Call," "Who?" and the perennial "Alexander's Ragtime Band." It was also the time of hip flasks and bathtub gin and bootleg booze "right off the boat," when young women affected short skirts and the "boyish form" or "flat chest-ed" look, when young men in bell bottom trousers and bril-liantined hair played the ukulele or, if they were clever enough, the banjo.... (Everyone knew Paul Whiteman's twelve-inch record of

27

[Walter] Donaldson's "At Sundown" with its "smooth" trumpet solo, which was regarded as "perfectly swell.") [1]

A good deal of this music was heard from a distance by the young necking in their cars in the dark privacy beyond the porch lights of the country club. (There were no radios in cars then.) Or

The Ziegfield Follies shows on Broadway in New York City were filled with music, jokes, and pretty women.

they heard it on the phonographs which they cranked by hand in the family living rooms (where they rolled up the rugs to dance) or on nickel-in-the-slot player pianos (the precursors of the ubiquitous juke boxes) in the short-order restaurants which began to dot the highways in the 1920s. In 1921 Americans bought more than 100 million gramophone records; they spent more money on them than on any other kind of recreation. Records all but put out of business the manufacturers of player pianos, which had been so popular in the first decade of the century and until the First World War, and which had introduced ragtime to so many people who would not have thought of going into the dubious emporiums where it was a steady diet. Almost all of the early jazz disks were sold as "race records," and they were aimed primarily at the Negro market. They were cheap to make (the musicians got about $5 each for a session, with $10 for the leader) and cheap to distribute. The first recordings of King Oliver; Bessie Smith, the great blues singer; Jelly Roll [Morton]; Louis Armstrong; and Duke Ellington were all sold as race records, "guaranteed to put you in a

---

[1] Almost all jazz, dance, and popular song records were ten-inch disks and lasted for about three minutes, a musical fact of life which played an important role in the shape of the music. Twelve-inch "popular" records were rare, though most "classical" music was on twelve-inchers, which lasted about six minutes.

dancing mood" and "tickle your toes." But they quickly jumped the borders of the Negro communities (which were not called "black ghettos" in those days) and spread by the millions everywhere....

Jazz evoked a moralistic counteroffensive much as ragtime had. It was regarded in strait-laced, middle-class, and predominantly Protestant circles as responsible for the ostensibly outrageous behavior and collapsing morals of the nation's youth. Since records had spread jazz everywhere and its low origins were not for a moment forgotten, it was looked upon in some quarters as a disease of epidemic proportions, a plague, indeed, a scourge.... Any popular music, no matter how watered down by polite jazz bands and crooners, male and female, if even remotely connected with the genuine article, was considered jazz, and was therefore deeply suspect.

AFTERWORD   Of course, the music called jazz, both real and watered down, survived and prospered. It became one of the most popular American exports to all continents. And behavior that seemed shocking in the 1920s would scarcely raise an eyebrow today.

Excerpts from "Blues, Boogie-Woogie, Swing" from **THE LIVELY AUDIENCE: A Social History of the Visual and Performing Arts in America, 1890–1950** by Russell Lynes. Copyright © 1985 by Russell Lynes. Reprinted by permission of HarperCollins Publishers.

INTRODUCTION   David Ewen has written many books about music. In the selection below from his volume *All the Years of American Popular Music*, he describes the amazing speed with which radio stations and radios multiplied and the new forms of entertainment this new device brought to people. Suddenly, they could listen to dance bands in their own homes and even hear the President talk to them in their kitchens. Franklin D. Roosevelt's use of this new instrument is discussed in "FDR and the New Deal" on pages 40–59. Can you think of some reasons why the radio spread so fast? Why did both bands and dance halls allow radio stations to broadcast their music for nothing?

Perspective 3

The Radio Invades the American Home

by David Ewen

I n the early twenties, radio started out as a crystal set toy for amateurs. By 1930, it had become a multimillion dollar industry, certainly the most powerful single entertainment medium. In 1922 the annual sale of radios amounted to sixty million dollars; by 1929 the figure was over eight hundred million dollars. The federal census revealed that over twelve million families owned radios, a radio in every third home.

Dr. Frank Conrad, an employee of Westinghouse Electric Company, conducted an all-important experiment in "wireless telephony" in a barn in East Pittsburgh early in 1920. In March of the same year, Lee De Forest installed a transmitter on the roof of the California Theater in San Francisco. Before the year was over, commercial broadcasts on a limited scale were initiated by the Detroit *News* using the call letters WWJ, and Westinghouse Broadcasting opened KDKA, a radio station in Pittsburgh, with the transmission of the Presidential election returns on November 2. After that, still in 1920, Westinghouse opened WJZ in Newark, New Jersey.

Radio passed directly from infancy to full maturity. In 1921, radio stations mushroomed so rapidly throughout the United States—by 1922 there were five hundred of them spread from one coast to the other—that the government had to step in and regulate the new industry by initiating the licensing of broadcasting stations. By the mid-1920s, over a thousand radio stations were in operation (a number reduced in 1927 to 708 by the newly instituted Federal Radio Commission whose mission was to control and regulate the airwaves). Rapid developments gave warning of the character radio broadcasting would eventually assume. Radio produced its

30

first singing stars on October 18, 1921, when Ernie Hare and Billy Jones, soon to become known as the "Happiness Boys," sang popular ballads, humorous songs and duets, and exchanged jokes for ninety minutes over WJZ to begin a radio career lasting eighteen years. They adopted "How Do You Do"...as their theme song, and during the twenties were responsible for making hits of several songs, among them "What Has Become of Hinky Dinky Parlay Voo?"...and "I Love to Dunk a Hunk of Sponge Cake."...

Radio swept the country in the 1920s and during the course of the decade radio receivers became a good deal easier to use than the one pictured here.

The first sponsored program appeared in 1922 when the Queensborough Corporation, a real estate outfit, presented a program over WEAF, New York, which at the same time introduced radio's first commercial. That year, radio also relayed for the first time an event from an outlying district remote from the studio by means of telephonic communication, when a New York station broadcast a football game from Chicago between the universities of Chicago and Princeton.

Radio announcing opened a new profession for performers in 1923 when Milton Cross, Ed Thorgenson and Phil Carlin served in that capacity for programs of the A & P Gypsies, starring Harry Horlick's orchestra over WEAF, New York, sponsored by the Great Atlantic and Pacific Tea Company. The first linking of several stations into a single chain was effected on November 3, 1924, to carry President Coolidge's speech over twenty-seven stations spanning the country. On November 15, 1926, the first radio network was formed, the National Broadcasting Company, an event commemorated with a gala program of serious and popular music as well as comedy, starring Will Rogers, Mary Garden, Weber and Fields, Titta Ruffo, Harold Bauer, the New York Symphony and the Oratorio Society of New York under Walter Damrosch, all broadcasting from newly opened studios in New York. Henceforth, it was possible to bring an entertainer to an audience of many millions during a single broadcast.

Necessity was the mother of the inventions that served as guidelines for early broadcasting. Since most of the small radio stations

Up in little Plymouth, Vermont, President Calvin Coolidge's father and his neighbors listened to his son's speech accepting the nomination of the Republican party in 1924.

had limited funds, they had to seek out programs calling for no payment. Thus microphones were set up in hotels, dance halls and other places in which dance bands appeared; both the bands and the auditoriums cooperated gladly for the sake of the publicity involved. The first remote radio pickup of a dance band took place in 1921 with regular broadcasts from Hotel Pennsylvania in New York of Vincent Lopez and his orchestra, a development largely responsible for this band's early successes in New York. In 1923, the music of Ben Bernie and his orchestra was picked up by remote from the Roosevelt Hotel. Fred Waring and his Pennsyl-vanians made their first broadcast in 1924 over WWJ in Detroit, and Paul Whiteman and his Orchestra were sponsored for a regular radio series in the mid-1920s. Rudy Vallee and his Yale Collegians had their performances at the Heigh-Ho Club in New York, broadcast over WABC, then a local station in New York.

Radio in the twenties brought fame not only to bands but also to many singers and many songs.

AFTERWORD   The radio remained the principal way to listen to music, news, soap operas, and other entertainments until the rapid rise of television in the 1950s and 1960s. Still, radio programs carrying music, news, drama, and talk shows reach more Americans than ever before as they drive to work in their automobiles or jog across the countryside wearing their Walkmans™.

From the book, ALL THE YEARS OF AMERICAN POPULAR MUSIC by David Ewen © 1977. Used by permission of the publisher, Prentice Hall/A division of Simon & Schuster, Englewood Cliffs, New Jersey.

INTRODUCTION   The rage for social dancing began shortly before World War I. Ragtime made dancing easier and less strenuous than older fast dances like the polka and the slightly slower schottische. But as writer Paula Fass shows in the excerpt below from her book *The Damned and the Beautiful: American Youth in the 1920's*, a great era of social dancing came with the 1920s and with the music often incorrectly called jazz. What was the main purpose of dancing for the young? Why did their elders often disapprove?

Perspective 4

Symbols of Liberation

*by **Paula S. Fass***

In the twenties, young men and women danced whenever the opportunity presented itself. Unquestionably the most popular social pastime, dancing was, of all potentially questionable and morally related behaviors, the least disreputable in the view of the young. For most youths dancing was not even questionable but a thoroughly respectable and almost compulsory form of socializing. Even at denominational schools, where dancing continued to be regarded as morally risky by officials, students clamored for a relaxation of the older bans as they asked officials to give up outdated "prejudiced feelings" and respond to "the bending of current public opinion." A dance was an occasion. It was a meeting ground between young men and women. It was a pleasurable recreation. But above all it was a craze.

The dancers were close, the steps were fast, and the music was jazz. And because popular forms of dancing were intimate and contorting, and the music was rhythmic and throbbing, it called down upon itself all the venom of offended respectability. Administrative officials as well as women's clubs and city fathers found the dancing provocative and indecent and tried at least to stop the young from engaging in its most egregious forms, if not from the dances entirely. But the young kept on dancing.

They started during the war years, and they danced through the decade. Dancing would leave its stamp on the twenties forever, and jazz would become the lingering symbol for an era. But whatever its symbolic value during the twenties and thereafter, dancing and jazz were forms of recreation, even a means of peer-group communication, that youth appropriated to itself. Dancing was, in the words of one survey of student life, the "chief social diversion of college men and women," and school officials unanimously acknowledged that

33

Dancing was so popular by the 1920s that couples like these in Culver City, California, even competed for prizes in "marathons" to see who could keep dancing for the longest time.

it was the most popular and universally indulged social activity. Almost all fraternity and university social affairs revolved around mixed dancing. Advertisements for dancing instruction appeared in most college papers. At the high schools, too, dancing was a prime occasion for socializing. One simply had to know how to dance to be sociable, and to be popular one had to know how to dance well. The ability to dance was both a sign of belonging to the world of youth and a necessary accomplishment if one wished to take part in the activities of that world....

The dances the young enjoyed most were the ones most criticized by adults. The shimmy and the toddle, which had become popular during the war, started the decade and the young on their dancing way. They were followed by the collegiate, the charleston, the black bottom, the tango. The dances brought the bodies and faces of the partners too dangerously close for the comfort of the

34

older folks. Dimmed lights added to the mood. Because of the novelty of the rhythms and the "indecent" motions involved, most of the adverse comments came at the beginning of the decade. As the era progressed, less was said, but not because the dancing stopped. The dancing went on, probably becoming more and not less popular and certainly more hectic. While the steps changed in fad fashion and increased in variety, they remained basically the same—exciting, sensuous, and always to the accompaniment of jazz. The older generation was no less opposed, but by working through the public opinion of the young they found a means of controlling what they considered its most indecent extremes. The young tempered the extremes to meet the adult criticism, but they were really calling the tune.

AFTERWORD   Dancing remained extremely popular through the thirties and forties as people thronged the dance halls and gyrated to bands big and small. Since those years the big "name" bands that used to tour the country, like Benny Goodman's or Tommy Dorsey's, playing at large dance halls have disappeared and the dance halls have closed. But, of course, dancing goes on, to small orchestras or recorded music, in discotheques, in clubs, hotels, and homes.

INTRODUCTION   In the selection below from jazz expert Ben Sidran's *Black Talk*, he explains how jazz moved from South to North. One of the major figures in this move, and in the history of jazz, was Louis Armstrong, who was born in New Orleans in 1900 and died in New York City in 1971. Armstrong was a poor boy who learned to play the cornet while he was in the New Orleans Colored Waifs' Home where he had been sent after a minor scrape with the police. Then he worked at a variety of jobs and studied music with Joe "King" Oliver. Armstrong arrived in Chicago in 1922. What was different about Armstrong's music? What did Armstrong and other southern musicians have to teach northern blacks?

Perspective 5

The Jazz Age

by **Ben Sidran**

Although he was not the first New Orleans musician to reach Chicago, Louis Armstrong was most notable for the equipoise, the visceral balance between Western and Negro musical styles of his playing. Perhaps no one walked the fence between the two cultures better than he did. Like [Buddy] Bolden before him, Armstrong was an innovator whose influence seemed single-handedly to reform black music. The balance of intellectual and emotional content in his playing impressed a vast and integrated audience. Armstrong combined the oral approach to rhythm and vocalization with an intuitive grasp of Western harmonic structure, creating a new synthesis acceptable to both blacks and whites.

Even as a young man, Armstrong was unlike other trumpet players in the way he incorporated Western harmonies with the blues. One local musician recalled, "I was the 'Blues King' of New Orleans, and when Louis played that day he played more blues than I ever heard in my life. It never did strike my mind that blues could be interpreted so many different ways. Every time he played a chorus it was different and you knew it was blues."

The variety of Armstrong's blues was a result of the imposition of chord substitutions on the minimal blues format, not a strictly worked out assault on Western harmonic structure but an evolved, intuitive manipulation of what information was available to an "unschooled" musician. Although in later life he learned how to read music, his understanding of Western harmonic structure was originally a function of what he heard, of his ability to play "by ear"

36

and "hear" the logic of harmonic structure at an often subconscious, or perhaps preconscious, level. Relying on the ability to read music implies a rigid *preconception* whereas playing "by ear" is part of the more free-flowing oral tradition and is merely *conception*. Hence, a musician can always learn to read music but, as is well known, even some of the best readers, i.e., the Western classical musicians, cannot "fake it," or improvise on a given body of material. One cannot be taught how to improvise black musical idioms, because the *theory* of improvisation develops through the *doing* of it. The act *is* the theory. Armstrong, it has been said, proved the idea that "if you can't sing it, you can't play it," that improvisation is based on the ability to "hear" with internal ears the sound of an internal voice. This reliance on "internal hearing" is part of the more general approach of the oral orientation, and indeed, Armstrong's horn playing sounded remarkably like his singing.

Armstrong's distinctly sophisticated—one could even say *rational*—version of the blues was almost fully developed before he reached Chicago where it came to fruition. His immigration to that city was part of the greater cultural migration of the period, part, too, of the general trend, which continues today, of blues innovation and techniques flowing from South to North.

Armstrong's immigration and subsequent success became part of the black social legend wherein the "bad nigger" had to leave the South and prove his manhood in the North, a process finally reversed during the sixties when the "bad niggers" like Stokely Carmichael became the first generation to return to the South. Ironically, the Southern musicians not only had to deal with the education of white audiences in the North, but also had to reintegrate much of the black population into the oral tradition.

Louis Armstrong is considered one of the greatest innovators in the history of jazz. This photograph was taken in the 1920s, when he first began to thrill audiences in Chicago and New York with his trumpet.

Louis Armstrong first came to Chicago to play in King Oliver's Creole Jazz Band. In this picture Armstrong is center with Oliver next to him on the right. The pianist, Lil Hardin, who later became Armstrong's wife, was a skilled musician in her own right.

Armstrong himself recalls his surprise at discovering the validity of this trend. "We watched close to see what their music would be like," he remembers of his first exposure to Northern Negro jazz musicians, "because we knew they had a big reputation in St. Louis and naturally, we were interested to see how our New Orleans bands, like Kid Ory's and the rest, would stack up against them. Well, we were surprised. In no time at all we could tell they were doing things that had been done down home years before. The leader would try to swing them away from the score but they didn't seem to know how." The Northern blacks could read music, but they couldn't "swing away from the score" or "fake it." This ability relied on exposure to the oral tradition, which was diluted or altogether lacking in Northern cities. In areas of recent black migration, such as Chicago or Kansas City, the problem was not as severe as it was in St. Louis or New York, which had older, more established black communities. It can be suggested that this is the main

38

reason why jazz "grew up" in Chicago and, later, Kansas City, but generally "passed through" New York and, to a lesser extent, St. Louis. In fact, the blues did not take root in New York until the late forties. Those areas with black populations fresh from the South drew their cultural security from Southern traditions; hence the importance of Chicago in the twenties.

AFTERWORD   Jazz has continued to grow and change in the years since Louis Armstrong began to play in Chicago. It is now popular around the world. Many jazz musicians from the United States have lived and practiced their art in Europe, and many Europeans are now expert in that idiom. Though Armstrong never lived abroad, recordings of his horn and voice were important in making jazz a synonym for America. On a hugely successful concert tour of Central and Eastern Europe in 1965, Armstrong was welcomed by large crowds, and in Budapest, Hungary, he thrilled 100,000 people with his brilliant and joyful playing and singing.

AMERICAN MUSIC IN THE JAZZ AGE

Perspectives on

FDR AND THE LEGACY OF THE NEW DEAL

The Great Depression of the 1930s touched the lives of all Americans as much as a natural disaster or a great war. While there were no battle-front casualties, there was every other kind of misery. The rich lost their fortunes, the middle class lost their comforts, the poor lost their jobs and went hungry. It is not surprising then that all Americans felt a desperate need to fight the evils that seemed everywhere. The New Deal was the name for the battle plan, and President Franklin D. Roosevelt the leader. The battlefront was in the long bread lines of the unemployed, on the farms where crops could not be sold, in stores where there were no customers, in homes lost to banks by people who could not pay their mortgages. Just as earlier Americans had disagreed over the tactics of their respected military leaders—Washington, Grant, Lee, and Pershing—so now there were conflicting opinions of the battle strategy of the New Deal, and the qualities of the commanding officer.

After the Great Depression, most United States citizens would never again believe that the least government was the best government.

Franklin D. Roosevelt was America's first "radio President." From his office in the White House, he talked to the people and raised their spirits.

41

With the New Deal—even before, with President Herbert Hoover—Americans realized that the federal government had far-reaching responsibilities to promote the welfare of all its citizens, and especially those most in need.

The so-called "welfare state" in the United States had its birth with the New Deal, and it has continued (with fluctuations) through all the administrations since, Republican as well as Democratic. Social Security, unemployment insurance, minimum wage laws, subsidies for farmers, and many other familiar measures all had their beginnings in the New Deal. Though there was some retreat from government activism by Presidents Eisenhower and Carter, the resistance was strongest under President Reagan. But while Reagan wanted to rein in and reduce the activities of the federal government, even he insisted that it was necessary to retain a safety net of programs to aid the old, the poor, and the unemployed.

Roosevelt tried to make conversation with an unhappy Herbert Hoover as they rode together to FDR's inauguration in 1933.

Ronald Reagan succeeded in shrinking government activity somewhat, but in his support of the safety net an essential part of the New Deal approach survived. And in perhaps the greatest compliment to Roosevelt and the New Deal, in his public addresses Reagan often referred to FDR and echoed his phrases. He used so much material from FDR's speeches in his acceptance of the Republican nomination in 1980 that the *New York Times* called him "Franklin Delano Reagan."

Reagan clearly wanted to dismantle much of the legacy of the New Deal. But he did so, he said, to save the rest: "Like FDR, may I say, I'm not trying to destroy what is best in our system of humane, free government—I'm doing everything I can to save it: to slow down the destructive rate of growth in taxes and spending; to prune nonessential programs so that enough resources will be left to meet the requirements of the truly needy." So it appeared that even those who wanted a smaller, less active government could not escape or deny the long and continuing influence of FDR and his New Deal.

In the excerpts that follow, you will find different views of Franklin D. Roosevelt and the New Deal. While each of the authors interprets the legacy of FDR and the New Deal in a different way, you will note that all refer to his ability to communicate with and lead the American people.

INTRODUCTION   Sir Isaiah Berlin is a world-renowned British philosopher and historian who was born in Riga, Latvia. The selection that follows is from a speech he made on the tenth anniversary of Roosevelt's death. In it Berlin singles out what he views as FDR's major accomplishments. What does he believe was Franklin Roosevelt's greatest service to a world demoralized by the depression? What other achievements of Roosevelt's does he single out?

Perspective 1

Roosevelt Through European Eyes

*by **Sir Isaiah Berlin***

No man made more public enemies, yet no man had a right to take greater pride in the quality and the motives of some of those enemies. He could justly call himself the friend of the people, and although his opponents accused him of being a demagogue, this charge seems to me unjust. He did not sacrifice fundamental political principles to a desire to retain power; he did not whip up evil passions merely in order to avenge himself upon those whom he disliked or wished to crush, or because it was an atmosphere in which he found it convenient to operate.

He saw to it that his administration was in the van of public opinion and drew it on instead of being dragged by it. He made the majority of his fellow citizens prouder to be Americans than they had been before. He raised their status in their own eyes, and in those of the rest of the world. It was an extraordinary transformation of an individual. Perhaps it was largely brought about by the collapse of his health in the early twenties, and his marvelous triumph over his disabilities. For he began life as a well-born, polite, agreeable, debonair, not particularly gifted young man, something of a prig, liked but not greatly admired by his contemporaries at Groton and at Harvard, a competent Assistant Secretary of the Navy in the First World War; in short, he seemed embarked on the routine career of an American patrician with moderate political ambitions. His illness and the support and encouragement and political qualities of his wife—whose greatness of character and goodness of heart history will duly record—seemed to transfigure his public personality into the strong and beneficent champion who became the father of his people, in an altogether unique fashion.

He was more than this: it is not too much to say that he altered the fundamental concept of government.... The welfare state, so

President Roosevelt, second from left, and Prime Minister Churchill met in Quebec in 1944 to discuss military strategy. On the left is the Earl of Athlone, governor general of Canada, and on the right Canada's Prime Minister MacKenzie King.

much denounced, has obviously come to stay: the direct moral responsibility for minimum standards of living and social services which it took for granted, are today accepted almost without murmur by the most conservative politicians in the Western democracies. The Republican Party in 1952 made no effort to upset the basic principles—which seemed utopian in the twenties—of Mr. Roosevelt's social legislation.

But Mr. Roosevelt's greatest service to mankind (after ensuring victory against the enemies of freedom) consists in the fact that he showed that it is possible to be politically effective and yet benevolent and civilized: that the fierce left and right wing propaganda of the thirties, according to which the conquest and retention of polit-

44

ical power is not compatible with human qualities, but necessarily demands from those who pursue it seriously the sacrifice of their lives upon the altar of some ruthless ideology, or the systematic practice of despotism—this propaganda, which filled the art and talk of the day, was simply untrue. Mr. Roosevelt's example strengthened democracy everywhere—that is to say, the view that the promotion of social justice and individual liberty does not necessarily mean the end of all efficient government; that power and order are not identical with a strait jacket of doctrine, whether economic or political; that it is possible to reconcile individual liberty and a loose texture of society with the indispensable minimum of organization and authority. And in this belief lies what Mr. Roosevelt's greatest predecessor once described as the last best hope on earth.

"Roosevelt's example strengthened democracy everywhere."

AFTERWORD   Although Berlin's speech was made in 1955, his foresight was accurate. Even our most conservative recent President, Ronald Reagan, admired FDR and followed him in some ways. And with the collapse of communism in many countries, it may be argued that FDR's defense of capitalism and democracy during the depression allowed the United States to remain an example and a beacon of hope to many lands long after Isaiah Berlin spoke.

Perspective 2

Roosevelt's Leadership

*by **Edgar Eugene Robinson***

Franklin D. Roosevelt shaped the history of his country... because he always appeared to be affirmative. He proclaimed the affirmative attitude to be all-important. To the American people in despondency after a period of dis-illusionment he said we can and will succeed!... And the magic rested in the fact that speaking with such assurance of objectives and not of obstacles, he reflected precisely what his hearers wished to hear....

Roosevelt's leadership resulted in fundamental changes in the government itself: in tremendous concentration of power in the Executive; in building up a vast system of bureaucratic control of private business; and by adding direct economic support of the citizen to the careful adjustment of conflicting economic interests in a free enterprise system....

By all tests he was a successful politician, the most successful of his day, if what is meant thereby is the manipulation of men, organizations, and programs to the end that the politician and his followers may remain in power. This was all-important if the politician was to take office away from the conservative and keep it out of the hands of the radical. Such a politician, in the course of his ceaseless activity, does accomplish much good, arouse much enthusiasm, and bring to his support millions.

But in terms of the ultimate solution of problems, or of placing such problems in the general stream of American development, he does incalculable harm. The American people accepted the pattern which was gradually woven by Roosevelt's leadership, and on the face of things millions profited from his action. But as the years passed, it became evident that the balance had to be paid....

During the years of his all-powerful leadership, Franklin Roosevelt made great decisions that tower above all others in their

influence upon the events of his time. Each of these decisions at the time either expressed the view of the majority of the American people, or appealed to them as desirable when the decision became known.

Certainly the majority of Americans wanted no co-operation with the defeated Hoover in the period of the interregnum.[1] Yet the results were disastrous at the time and in the years that followed....

That the majority hailed with enthusiasm the expenditure of public funds for relief, public works, and the vast plan of public utilities has been self-evident. Thus the nation was embarked on a long program of deficit spending resulting in inflation and the constant threat of national bankruptcy.

Building the dams of the Tennessee Valley Authority put thousands to work in the 1930s and 1940s. This realistic painting by Paul Sample shows the Norris Dam under construction.

---

[1] The interregnum was the period from the November election until the President took office on March 4. The 20th Amendment, ratified in 1933, shortened this period by changing the inauguration date to January 20. In the nation's early days, travel was so slow and difficult that extra time was needed between the election and the inauguration. With the Great Depression, four months seemed far too long to wait for action from the new President.

FDR AND THE LEGACY OF THE NEW DEAL

FDR, seated on the left in the open touring car, was greeted with enthusiasm when he visited a Civilian Conservation Corps camp at Bear Mountain, New York, in 1933.

So, too, the people as a whole applauded President Roosevelt's attempt to curb the Supreme Court and thus to do away with the testing of the "New Deal" under the Constitution of the United States....

Franklin Delano Roosevelt appeared in a great role on a vast stage, a hero not only to millions of his fellow countrymen, but also to millions of his contemporaries throughout the world. The role was tragic in a fateful drama—a man of fundamentally good intention overwhelmed by the forces of his time in a gigantic struggle to solve the pressing problems of his nation,.... President Roosevelt was a leader in a revolution...a rearrangement of social and economic forces and a change of the function of government in American life.... The means he used...to implement his ideas appear in terms of their development under his skillful and adroit direction. The struggle in the final analysis seems to be primarily one of intellectual grasp and moral discrimination. Roosevelt's failure lay in his unsuccessful attempt to justify the means or establish the ends he had in view. This was his personal tragedy. Inasmuch as on major decisions he had a majority support, it was also the tragedy of the American people.

AFTERWORD   Many historians today would not agree with Robinson's analysis of FDR's Presidency. There is no question that Roosevelt expanded the powers of the Presidency and the federal government substantially. Some critics feel that Roosevelt did not go far enough—that he had an opportunity to make radical changes, and did not. Others feel that he went just about far enough. There is a third group, however, who still agrees with Robinson.

INTRODUCTION   Daniel J. Boorstin, historian, teacher, Pulitzer prize-winning author, Librarian of Congress Emeritus, is co-editor of this volume. In this excerpt from his book *Hidden History*, he analyzes the means used by FDR to reach and lead the people. What possible dangers does Boorstin see in these techniques and devices?

———— ❦ ————

Perspective 3

A Nationally Advertised President

*by **Daniel J. Boorstin***

F DR was our first "nationally advertised" President. The attitude of the vast majority of the American people to him was as different from that of their grandfathers to the Presidents of their day as our attitude to General Motors is different from that of our great-grandfathers to the village harness maker. Like other "nationally advertised brands," FDR could not, of course, have been successful if he had not had something to offer. But he might not have been able to sell himself to the American public on such a scale, and for twice as many terms as any of his predecessors, without the aid of certain revolutionary changes in our system of public communication....

By the time Franklin Delano Roosevelt came into office on March 4, 1933, technological and institutional innovations had in many ways prepared the way for a transformation of the relation between President and people. Communications from the President to the reading or listening public, which formerly had been ceremonial, infrequent, and addressed to small audiences, could now be constant, spontaneous, and directed to all who could read or hear (sometimes whether they wished to or not). And now through the questions put to the President at his regular press conferences, and through the telegrams and mail received after his radio addresses or public statements, he could sense the temper and gauge the drift of public opinion and so discover what the sovereign people wanted. He could even send up trial balloons to get some advance idea of public response to his future decisions. The President was no longer simply dealing with the "people," but with "public opinion."

There is no denying that FDR possessed a genius for using these means of communication. Without them he could hardly have developed that novel intimacy between people and President which marked his administrations. In the little memorial miscellany published by Pocket Books on April 18, 1945 (less than a week

49

The radio brought Franklin D. Roosevelt's fireside chats into living rooms and kitchens across America.

after FDR's death), we read in Carl Carmer's verse dialogue:

Woman:
... Come home with me
If you would think of him. I never saw him—
But I knew him. Can you have forgotten
How, with his voice, he came into our house,
The President of these United States,
Calling us friends....
Do you remember how he came to us
That day twelve years ago—a little more—
And you were sitting by the radio
(We had it on the kitchen table then)
Your head down on your arms as if asleep.

For the first time in American history the voice of the President was a voice from kitchen tables, from the counters of bars and lunchrooms, and the corners of living rooms.

FDR's relaxed and informal style, both in writing and speaking, enabled him to make the most of the new informal circumstances under which people heard him. That he was compelled by his infirmity to sit while giving his radio talks only added to the informality. A whole world separates FDR's speeches from those of his immediate predecessors—from the stilted rhetoric of the oratory collected in such volumes as Calvin Coolidge's *Foundations of the Republic* (1926) or Herbert Hoover's *Addresses upon the American Road* (1938). Earlier Presidential speeches had too often echoed the style and sentiments of commencement addresses; FDR could say something informal and concrete even in such an unpromising State Paper as a Mother's Day Proclamation.

Perhaps never before had there been so happy a coincidence of personal talent with technological opportunity as under his administrations. In the eight volumes of the *Public Papers and Addresses of Franklin D. Roosevelt*, which cover the era of the New Deal, we discover two new genres of political literature which were the means by which a new relationship between President and people

50

was fashioned. The first genre was established in transcriptions of Presidential press conferences; the second, in FDR's radio talks, the "fireside chats." Both are distinguished by an engaging casualness and directness; but this is not all that makes them new genres in the literature of American politics. Here, for the first time among Presidential papers, we find an extensive body of public utterances that are unceremonious yet serious.

…While later Presidents might lack the vividness of FDR's personality, perhaps never again would any man attain the Presidency or discharge its duties satisfactorily without entering into an intimate and conscious relation with the whole public. This has opened unprecedented opportunities for effective and enlightening leadership—with unprecedented temptations. For never before has it been so easy for a statesman to seem to lead millions while in reality tamely echoing their every shifting mood and inclination.

AFTERWORD   While it appears that the American people have not yet had a leader who merely followed their moods and inclinations, the threat has not lessened. It may, in fact, even have grown greater since Roosevelt's day as national polling on every subject imaginable has become an almost daily event. In addition, Presidents have become adroit in manipulating television for their own purposes. Since most people now get their news from TV instead of the written word, this has increased a President's ability to seem to lead while actually only following.

INTRODUCTION   The selection below is excerpted from *The Progressive Presidents: Roosevelt, Wilson, Roosevelt, Johnson* by John Morton Blum, the Woodward Professor of History at Yale University. Blum puts Franklin D. Roosevelt in the tradition and under the influence of the Progressive Era of approximately 1900–1920 during which Theodore Roosevelt and Woodrow Wilson greatly increased the power of the Presidency and the federal government. But Franklin Roosevelt went beyond the earlier progressives. What, according to Blum, were some of the lasting changes that FDR brought about?

Perspective 4

Franklin Roosevelt

*by **John Morton Blum***

Like the progressives before him, Franklin Roosevelt intended from the beginning of the New Deal to save capitalism by reforming it. His liberalism, like theirs, had middle-class origins and goals. The New Deal moved far beyond the perimeters of earlier progressive striving. Agriculture, public utilities, the airlines and the truckers, the coal and oil industries, the banks and exchanges all felt the bite of federal authority. The success of the union movement and the enactment in peacetime of potentially redistributive revenue legislation [taxes that would change the distribution of wealth] gave the New Deal an egalitarian cast that most progressives would have resented. Yet the New Deal was radical if at all, in its scope, not in its purpose. Roosevelt reduced the risks upon which capitalism had often floundered and endeavored to enlarge the middle class and to ease access to it because those objectives infused his most enduring priorities. They explained the cryptic statement with which he described himself: "I am that kind of liberal because I am that kind of conservative."

Within the constraints imposed by the Depression, the New Deal encouraged long-standing American aspirations to own a farm or home, and to acquire a useful education and dignified employment. The economic bill of rights that Roosevelt pronounced in 1944 as part of his postwar program incorporated those aspirations. It included rights to a "useful and remunerative" job, to decent housing and to a good education, as well as to protection from the financial fears of old age, accident, sickness, and unemployment. The wartime GI bill delivered the substance of those rights to veterans, the only Americans to whom Congress was yet willing to

52

extend Roosevelt's "new goals of happiness and well-being."

During both depression and war the President and his associates also recruited members of previously proscribed ethnic groups to elite positions in government and politics. Progressivism had attracted and relied upon a disproportionate number of white Prot-estant Americans, though by the early twentieth century and increasingly thereafter immigrants and second-generation Americans were gaining a growing voice within the Democratic party in the cities. To strengthen their allegiance the New Dealers unabashedly practiced recognition politics. Especially in the industrial states, the Democrats during the 1930's and 1940's ran balanced tickets characterized by the presence on them of Irish and Jewish candidates, often also of Italians or Poles. Without lowering previous standards of quality, Roosevelt also regularly drew from those and similar groups for appointment to the federal judiciary, to other major federal offices, and to the new agencies and informal councils of the New Deal. In so doing he reached into fresh reservoirs of talent and sensibility. Outsiders in American society understood their own problems better than did most old-stock observers. The President needed the ablest among those outsiders to devise and manage programs suitable to his purposes.

Eleanor Roosevelt pushed her husband to expand the recognition of women and blacks, long the victims of Washington's hostility or indifference. The Women's Bureau of the Democratic party drew women into politics. Roosevelt made Frances Perkins his secretary of labor, the first woman ever to join the cabinet. Within her domain and particularly also in Harry Hopkins', strong women, most of them alert to the special social problems of their sex, assumed responsible federal posts. Though their number seemed small by the standards of a later generation, Roosevelt went far beyond any of his predecessors in placing women in government. Blacks fared less well, partly because southern senators approved appointments only of their regional friends to federal offices in the southern states, including offices overseeing work relief which reached distressingly few southern blacks. Yet Roosevelt ended the lily-white practices of Republican administrations of the 1920's; New Dealers terminated the segregation of facilities within federal buildings in Washington, and at least a token coterie of black

Eleanor Roosevelt's energy and activity set a new standard for First Ladies. In this photograph she is talking to Mary McLeod Bethune at the National Conference on Problems of the Negro and Negro Youth.

Robert C. Weaver, a Ph.D. in economics from Harvard, was one of a number of black professionals appointed to important positions by FDR.

administrators reached influential positions. More important, in northern cities blacks received close to an equitable share of work relief and by 1936 most urban blacks, recipients also of favor from local Democratic leaders, had moved into the party of the New Deal. By 1940 blacks constituted a significant element within the Democratic coalition.

The New Deal did not complete the democratization of American political life; it did hasten that process. It did not remove prejudice from government; it did reduce it. Roosevelt neither started nor joined movements for equal rights for women or blacks. Those causes stood low in his order of priorities which put recovery and reform to the front until 1940, and victory above all else during the war. But Roosevelt and the New Deal gladly accepted the pluralism of American society and tempered the elitism of early century reformers by making the search for able governors continually inclusive instead of usually exclusive. The President attracted a constituency more varied than most progressives ever solicited and brought to the federal establishment, which he so happily expanded, a company of men and women from backgrounds as diverse as American society itself.

AFTERWORD   By his policy of inclusion, rather than exclusion, and by his awareness of certain people's needs, Franklin Delano Roosevelt created a coalition of supporters—blacks, immigrants, Catholics, Jews, union members, and many others (largely from the cities)—who would have elected him, it has been observed, to a fifth and even a sixth term as easily as they did to a fourth. And when they could no longer vote for Roosevelt, they continued to vote for Democrats for Congress. Though the old Roosevelt coalition has often splintered since, especially over the Presidency, the Democratic hold on Congress has been remarkably strong.

This selection is reprinted from THE PROGRESSIVE PRESIDENTS: Roosevelt, Wilson, Roosevelt, Johnson by John Morton Blum, by permission of W.W. Norton & Company, Inc. Copyright © 1980 by W.W. Norton & Company, Inc.

INTRODUCTION   Barton J. Bernstein is a professor of history at Stanford University. The selection below is from his essay in his collection *Towards a New Past: Dissenting Essays in American History*. Bernstein is considered to be a "New Left" historian, that is, one who, under the influence of the 1960s' radical movements, approaches American history with a Marxist or other leftist position. What does he identify as the failures of the New Deal? What does he think FDR should have done? Did the New Deal accomplish anything?

—❦—

Perspective 5

The New Deal: The Conservative Achievements of Liberal Reform

by Barton J. Bernstein

Enamored of Franklin D. Roosevelt and recalling the bitter opposition to welfare measures and restraints upon business, many liberal historians have emphasized the New Deal's discontinuity with the immediate past. For them there was a "Roosevelt Revolution," or at the very least a dramatic achievement of a beneficent liberalism which had developed in fits and spurts during the preceding three decades.... The New Deal has generally commanded their approval for such laws or institutions as minimum wages, public housing, farm assistance, the Tennessee Valley Authority, the Wagner Act, more progressive taxation, and social security. For most liberal historians the New Deal meant the replenishment of democracy, the rescuing of the federal government from the clutches of big business, the significant redistribution of political power. Breaking with laissez faire, the new administration, according to these interpretations, marked the end of the passive or impartial state and the beginning of positive government, of the interventionist state acting to offset concentrations of private power, and affirming the rights and responding to the needs of the unprivileged.

...[T]hese themes no longer seem adequate to characterize the New Deal. The liberal reforms of the New Deal did not transform the American system; they conserved and protected American corporate capitalism, occasionally by absorbing parts of threatening programs. There was no significant redistribution of power in American society, only limited recognition of other organized groups, seldom of unorganized peoples. Neither the bolder programs advanced by New Dealers nor the final legislation greatly extended the beneficence of government beyond the middle classes or drew upon the wealth of the few for the needs of the many.

55

While the New Deal raised spirits and provided many people with temporary jobs, it was not able to end the depression and put everyone to work.

Designed to maintain the American system, liberal activity was directed toward essentially conservative goals. Experimentalism was most frequently limited to means; seldom did it extend to ends. Never questioning private enterprise, it operated within safe channels, far short of Marxism or even of native American radicalisms that offered structural critiques and structural solutions.

All of this is not to deny the changes wrought by the New Deal—the extension of welfare programs, the growth of federal power, the strengthening of the executive, even the narrowing of property rights. But it is to assert that the elements of continuity are stronger, that the magnitude of change has been exaggerated. The New Deal failed to solve the problem of depression, it failed to raise the impoverished, it failed to redistribute in-come, it failed to extend equality and generally countenanced racial discrimination and segregation. It failed generally to make business more responsible to the social welfare or to threaten business's pre-eminent political power. In this sense, the New Deal, despite the shifts in tone and spirit from the earlier decade, was profoundly conservative and continuous with the 1920s.

AFTERWORD   New Left historians and other radicals felt frustrated by the New Deal. They thought that while Roosevelt had the opportunity to change radically the American system, he did not do so. They were bitter against Roosevelt for failing to seize his rare opportunity. Right-wing critics, of course, thought that FDR had transformed the nation into a welfare state.

From TOWARDS A NEW PAST: DISSENTING ESSAYS IN AMERICAN HISTORY by Barton J. Bernstein. Copyright © 1968 by Random House, Inc. Reprinted by permission of Pantheon Books, a division of Random House, Inc.

INTRODUCTION   William E. Leuchtenburg is William Rand Kenan Professor of History at the University of North Carolina, Chapel Hill. He is an expert on Franklin D. Roosevelt and the New Deal. The selection below is from his *In the Shadow of FDR: From Harry Truman to Ronald Reagan*. Why does he think it was so difficult to be a President following FDR?

Perspective 6

In the Shadow of FDR

*by **William E. Leuchtenburg***

Franklin D. Roosevelt proved to be an especially tough act to follow. In his more than three terms in the White House, he had become, as one writer has stated, "the Paul Bunyan of American Presidents: a myth based on vividly remembered reality." So large did he loom in the popular imagination that he even affected the reputations of those who had come before him. As one of Grover Cleveland's biographers has noted perceptively:

> Perhaps the harshest thing that happened to Cleveland was Franklin Roosevelt.... FDR's glowing presidential style and achievement cast shadows in all directions—forward to encompass each of his successors, and backward to measure every predecessor. Dexterity, innovation, and public compassion now became the main criteria for comparing presidents.... History insured that the linkage between Cleveland and FDR would be defined to Cleveland's disadvantage.

Much the same observation could have been made by the biographers of other presidents, certainly with respect to Herbert Hoover and even, or perhaps especially, to Woodrow Wilson.

Decades after his death, Roosevelt continued to cast a shadow. When Jimmy Carter campaigned in West Virginia in the midterm elections of 1978, pictures of FDR still adorned the walls of miners' shacks. In the 1980s millions of Americans still drew on the accomplishments of the Roosevelt years: old people counted on social security benefits; Southerners electrified their homes with TVA power; big-city residents lived in New Deal housing projects; New Yorkers crossed the Triboro Bridge and Virginians traveled the Skyline Drive. The jobs legislation enacted in 1983 owed an obvious debt to the WPA, and a bill to create a new program modeled on the CCC won wide support in Congress. Five miles from

This cartoon from 1946 shows the public, Uncle Sam, and President Truman all recalling FDR a year after his death.

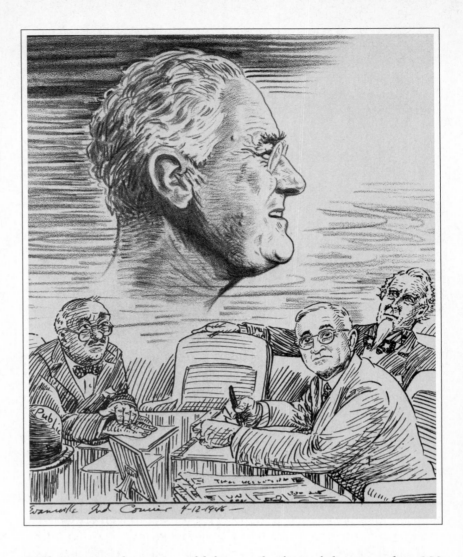

Willow, in southwestern Oklahoma, the first of the more than 200 million trees planted in FDR's pet project of a shelter belt against dust storms on the dry western plains still thrived. Some of the most prominent political figures of the 1980s looked back half a century for guideposts. Teddy Kennedy frequently alluded to FDR, while Fritz Mondale recalled having been raised in a family that regarded Franklin Roosevelt as a household god.

FDR's successors in the White House faced an imposing set of challenges. Their greatest problem with respect to their precursors was how to solve the question that troubles the artist—"What is there left to do?" Roosevelt had handed down a rich legacy of ideas and institutions to his successors. But by that very token he had also made it much less likely that their achievements would equal or surpass his. They had to cope, too, with a further demand—to remain loyal to FDR, as the Roosevelt idolators expected them to be, and yet to establish their own identity in order to create a record comparable to his. Ironically, the more faithful they were to FDR, the more unlike him they would be, for Roosevelt had made his place in history by diverging from the pattern of his predecessors. They could succeed by greatly enlarging what he had accomplished or by finding new fields of endeavor, neither of which was an easy task, or by departing from his legacy, an action fraught with difficulty, for it seemed a kind of filial disobedience.

AFTERWORD   Even Roosevelt's most conservative successor as President, Ronald Reagan, often used Franklin D. Roosevelt's name and copied his techniques. But Reagan's goals were very different. When he became President in 1980, he thought the government itself was the cause of most of the nation's problems. He wanted to diminish its size and decrease its activity. Reagan's amazing popularity during his two terms in office, even as he sought to reduce domestic programs, may have finally begun to diminish the long shadow of FDR.

Reprinted from William E. Leuchtenburg: In the Shadow of FDR: From Harry Truman to Ronald Reagan. Copyright © by Cornell University Press. Revised and Updated Chapter 8 © 1985, 1989 by Cornell University. Used by permission of the publisher, Cornell University Press.

FDR AND THE LEGACY OF THE NEW DEAL

Perspectives on

THE DECISION TO DROP THE ATOMIC BOMB

August 6, 1945, in Hiroshima, Japan, dawned sunny, hot, and humid. The city's air-raid sirens sounded at 7:09 A.M., but only a U.S. weather plane appeared, so the all-clear sounded at 7:31. It did not go off again when three B-29s (B-*san* or Mr. B., as the Japanese called them) were spotted on radar, since these also seemed too few for a raid.

The 330,000 people in the city were nervous. Somehow, as other large Japanese cities were destroyed by bombs and napalm, there had been little damage in Hiroshima. The citizens did not know that they were being saved for a major experiment—one that would demonstrate the power of an astonishing new weapon.

At 8:15 A.M. there was a blinding white flash and most of Hiroshima disappeared. Since there is uncertainty over how many died, you will read varying numbers in the selections that follow. But according to Richard Rhodes in *The Making of the Atomic Bomb* (1986), "Recent estimates place the number of deaths up to the end of 1945 at 140,000. The dying continued: five-year deaths related to the bomb reached 200,000." This

This watch stopped forever when the atomic bomb exploded over Hiroshima at 8:15 local time. Why the hour hand is slightly before, instead of slightly after, eight is a mystery.

61

was, as Rhodes observed, "an extraordinary density of killing." By comparison, the terrifying Tokyo firebombing raid of March 9 had killed 100,000 in a population of one million. To this day people continue to die from the long-term effects of the atomic bomb's radiation.

The news of the bombing was released to the American people the same day. This was the first they had heard of this terrible new weapon. It had been developed under such a dense cloud of secrecy that many high government officials (including the Vice-President and the Secretary of State) did not learn about it until after the event. Harry Truman was told of the work on the bomb only after he was sworn in as President.

Franklin D. Roosevelt had been alerted to the possibility of creating an atomic bomb in October 1939 when he was visited by economist Alexander Sachs who carried a letter from the world-renowned mathematician, Albert Einstein. Einstein implied that the Germans were already working on this fearsome weapon.

While government-funded research was undertaken on the bomb in the United States beginning in 1940, the major effort did not come until 1942. Referred to as the Manhattan Project (because some of the early research was done at Columbia University on Manhattan Island in New York), it employed 150,000 people at its peak. To create the basic materials needed for the bomb, two large new communities were built away from prying eyes, at Oak Ridge, Tennessee, and Hanford, Washington. New factories were constructed at these places to produce the uranium 238 and plutonium for the nuclear reaction in the hearts of the bombs.

Robert Oppenheimer (in hat) and other scientists measured radioactivity at this site in New Mexico two months after the first bomb was tested .

A secret laboratory was set up at Los Alamos, New Mexico, the location of a former private school in the Sangre de Cristo Mountains of New Mexico. There in the wilderness the scientists labored to figure ways to turn theory into reality. A fictional (and not entirely accurate) account of the work at Los Alamos may be seen in the 1989 movie *Fat Man and Little Boy* (the names given, respectively, to the bombs dropped on Nagasaki and Hiroshima).

In charge of the entire project was Roosevelt's reserved and aristocratic Secretary of War Henry L. Stimson, who had first served in that position from 1911 to 1913 under President Taft. In direct command of the

PERSPECTIVES

enterprise was Major General Leslie R. Groves, Jr., a professional army officer. Groves was hard-driving, difficult, and disliked by many who worked for him. But even his aide, who declared that he hated him, had to admit that he was "one of the most capable individuals I've ever met."

One of Groves's best decisions was to appoint J. Robert Oppenheimer, a physicist at the University of California at Berkeley, to head the Los Alamos laboratory. Groves did this over the objections of army intelligence which was convinced that Oppenheimer's associations with Communists made him untrustworthy. Oppenheimer proved to be a superb leader who inspired his scientists. One of his physicists remarked that instead of staying in his office, Oppenheimer "was present in the laboratory or in the seminar rooms when a new effect was measured, when a new idea was conceived."

As the work on the atomic bomb neared completion in 1945, but before the device had yet been tested, various committees began to consider the "control, organization, legislation, and publicity" of the bomb. One committee of scientists at the University of Chicago (where the first controlled chain reaction converting matter into energy had taken place in 1942) in late June 1945 came out strongly against dropping the new weapon on Japan without warning. They feared that the world, and especially the Soviet Union, would be "deeply shocked" by such a brutal act. The suspicions of "a nation which was capable of secretly preparing and suddenly releasing a weapon" of such indiscriminate power, the scientists feared, might make it ultimately impossible to abolish atomic bombs by international agreement.

This Chicago committee recommended instead that the power of the bomb should be demonstrated "before the eyes of representatives of all United Nations, on the desert or a barren island." This suggestion was not followed, according to Secretary Stimson, because it was uncertain that any given bomb would actually explode and a failure might encourage the Japanese to keep on fighting. On top of that, there were so few bombs (only two would be ready by August) that the government hesitated to waste one on a demonstration. Stimson believed that there might be over one million American casualties (killed, wounded, and missing in action) if it was necessary to invade Japan. If the bomb made that unnecessary, it might actually save American lives. Others, including General Eisenhower, thought that Japan would soon collapse. Still, fearful of Japanese troops—whose deadly tenaciousness had been proven on Iwo Jima, Okinawa, and other Pacific islands—the government decided to use the bomb against Japan as soon as possible. So the age of nuclear warfare began at Hiroshima on August 6, 1945.

THE DECISION TO DROP THE ATOMIC BOMB

INTRODUCTION   Clark Clifford is a lawyer who served as President Harry Truman's special counsel and succeeded Robert McNamara as Secretary of Defense under Lyndon Johnson. In the selection below from his memoirs as published in the *New Yorker* magazine in 1991, Clifford relates what he learned from Truman about the conclusion to use the atomic bomb. What was Truman's goal when he decided to drop the bomb? Was it meant to frighten the Soviets?

Perspective 1

The Decision to Drop the Bomb

by Clark Clifford

When President Truman and I became closer, he talked often about the decision to drop the atomic bomb on Japan. Although he never evinced any doubt about his decision, he wanted his actions to be understood. He always emphasized the point that no one had told him about the Manhattan Project before he became President. To withhold from the man next in the chain of command the most vital secret of the war was not an oversight but a deliberate—and, I believe, irresponsible—decision by President Roosevelt and his senior advisers.

President Truman told me he had first heard of the existence of "the most terrible weapon" on the evening he became President, less than four hours after Roosevelt died and only twenty minutes after being sworn in as President. Secretary of War Stimson had then taken him aside and told him that Roosevelt had set up a special organization to develop a "superbomb," which was almost ready for its first test. President Truman said he had been so overwhelmed by the events of the day that the information about the bomb did not sink in—a clear demonstration, if any were needed, of the need to keep the Vice-President fully informed of important events, so that he (or she) can deal with any decisions that need to be made quickly if the President is unable, for whatever reason, to perform his functions.

When Stimson heard nothing more on the subject from the new President for two weeks, he asked to see him "on a highly secret matter." He brought with him General Groves. They handed President Truman a detailed memorandum that contained a heart-stopping sentence: "Within four months we shall in all probability have completed the most terrible weapon ever known in human history, one bomb which could destroy a whole city."

This is the way that President Truman learned that he would soon face a decision unique in history, and would face it under very difficult conditions. While the men on whom he relied for advice had worked with each other for years, he knew what they now told him for only the first time. Given the number of other pressing matters with which he had to deal, he had no time to educate himself adequately. But from the moment he met with Stimson and Groves he understood that the final decision would have to be his, and his alone. "I am going to have to make a decision which no man in history has ever had to make," he said to the very next person he saw after Stimson left his office—Leonard Reinsch, a radio-station director who was temporarily assigned to the White House staff. "I'll make the decision, but it is terrifying to think about what I will have to decide."

When President Truman discussed these events later, he always made it clear that he had only one goal: to end the war as soon as possible. I stress this point because of the controversy that continues even today concerning three aspects of these events.

First, there has been speculation, over the years, that the use of the bomb against Japan instead of Germany was related to racial factors; that, not wishing to use it against Europeans, the United States reserved it for Asians. That notion is utterly false. The use of new techniques, such as incendiary bombing, against targets that included Dresden was nearly as devastating as the atomic bomb. Besides, the men who built the bomb, including J. Robert Oppenheimer, had hoped to finish it in time for it to be used against Germany. I have no doubt that if it had been finished in time to be useful in shortening the European war President Roosevelt or President Truman would have used it.

Secretary of War Stimson reported to President Truman in the Oval Office on the results of the atomic bombing of Hiroshima.

Second, a theory has frequently been advanced that one of the main reasons for the use of the bomb against Japan was to intimidate the Russians. As recently as late 1989, Eduard Shevardnadze, then the Soviet Foreign Minister, repeated this charge. "Militarily there was no need to drop nuclear bombs on Hiroshima and Nagasaki," he said in a speech in New York. "It was a political decision taken to intimidate us. This tragedy of the century must be brought to light and its perpetrators globally denounced." There is no evidence to support this theory.

THE DECISION TO DROP THE ATOMIC BOMB

Even the relatively small atomic bombs used against Japan in World War II could destroy entire cities. Only the strongest buildings remained standing and they had been gutted by fire.

Never did I hear President Truman or any of his colleagues discuss the use of the bomb against Japan in terms of Soviet-American relations. In the summer of 1945, when a weary nation and its new President wanted nothing more than to end the Pacific war quickly and bring the rest of the troops home, considerations of postwar strategy and relations with Moscow were low on the national agenda, and unrelated to the discussion of what to do with the new weapon.

Finally, there is the most frequently debated question about the decision to drop the bombs on Hiroshima and Nagasaki: Why did the President not order a demonstration bomb dropped on an unpopulated area before using one on a populated area?

To President Truman the issue was not as complicated as it seems to many people today. There were several reasons he did not consider the idea of a demonstration bomb. First, his scientists and military advisers, with only one test behind them, were not absolutely certain that the next bomb would perform properly, and they did not want to risk a publicized dud. Second, his advisers felt that Japan would not appreciate the uniqueness and the full destructive power of the bomb unless it was used against an actual target. The fact that the President was at Potsdam [Germany] or on the cruiser [sailing to Europe and returning] during the most critical period—between the flash in the New Mexico sky on July 16th and the flight of the Enola Gay on August 6th—meant that he was never presented with a full-scale argument for a demonstration bomb. He told me later, however, that he had considered it, and had come to the conclusion that a demonstration would not suffice after a war of such terrible carnage—that Japanese lives would have to be sacrificed to save many more lives, both American and Japanese.

In the end, what weighed most heavily with President Truman was the military estimate that enormous numbers of American casualties would be suffered in an assault upon the main islands of Japan. Only eight months earlier, the American Army had suffered heavy losses in the Battle of the Bulge, against a German enemy thought to have been already defeated. The assumption was that the Japanese, deeply committed to their emperor, would fight even more tenaciously than Germany, and everyone remembered that the Third Reich had resisted down to the last street in Berlin. In our conversations the President mentioned this factor more than any other. The estimate that stayed in his mind was a total of five hundred thousand, consisting of half killed in action and half wounded. Thus in President Truman's mind the decision was relatively simple—a choice between sacrificing a horrendous number of Americans and using a weapon that could shorten the war dramatically. Although he later spent considerable time defending his decision, he did not agonize over it at the time. Death and destruction on the most extreme scale had been the hallmarks of both the First World War, in which Harry Truman fought, and the one whose conclusion was now in his hands. He wanted to end the war as quickly as possible.

AFTERWORD   Harry Truman may not have agonized over the decision at the time, as writer Merle Miller observed in his *Plain Speaking: An Oral Biography of Harry S. Truman*, but "he had certainly given it a good deal of thought." Miller found in the Truman Library a book on the atom bomb which ended with the following lines from *Hamlet* carefully underlined by the President:

> …let me speak to the yet unknowing world
> How these things came about: So shall you hear
> Of carnal, bloody, and unnatural acts,
> Of accidental judgements, casual slaughters,
> Of deaths put on by cunning and forced cause,
> And, in this upshot, purposes mistook
> Fall'n on the inventors heads….
> But let this same be presently perform'd,
> Even while men's minds are wild; lest more mischance,
> On plots and errors, happen.

From SERVING THE PRESIDENT by Clark Clifford. Copyright © 1991 by Clark Clifford. Reprinted by permission of Random House Publishers, Inc.

THE DECISION TO DROP THE ATOMIC BOMB

INTRODUCTION   Immediately after Hiroshima was obliterated by the first atomic bomb, Dwight Macdonald, a radical and a pacifist, published a blistering editorial in his small journal *Politics* denouncing the act as immoral. What were his major points?

Perspective 2

The Bomb

*by **Dwight Macdonald***

At 9:15 [8:15 Japan time] on the morning of August 6, 1945, an American plane dropped a single bomb on the Japanese city of Hiroshima. Exploding with the force of 20,000 tons of TNT, the bomb destroyed in a twinkling two-thirds of the city, including, presumably, most of the 343,000 human beings who lived there. No warning whatsoever was given. This atrocious action places "us," the defenders of civilization, on a moral level with "them," the beasts of [the Nazi concentration camp] Maidanek. And "we," the American people, are just as much and as little responsible for this horror as "they," the German people.

So much is obvious. But more must be said. For the "atomic" bomb renders anticlimactical even the ending of the greatest war in history (which seems imminent as this goes to press). (1) THE CONCEPTS, "WAR" AND "PROGRESS," ARE NOW OBSOLETE. Both suggest human aspirations, emotions, aims, consciousness. "The greatest achievement of organized science in history," said President Truman after the Hiroshima catastrophe—which it probably was, and so much the worse for organized science. Such "progress" fills no human needs of either the destroyed or the destroyers. And a war of atomic bombs is not a war. It is a scientific experiment. (2) THE FUTILITY OF MODERN WARFARE SHOULD NOW BE CLEAR. Must we not now conclude, with [philosopher] Simone Weil, that the technical aspect of war today is the evil, regardless of political factors? Can one imagine that the atomic bomb could ever be used "in a good cause"? Do not such means instantly, of themselves, corrupt ANY cause? (3) ATOMIC BOMBS ARE THE NATURAL PRODUCT OF THE KIND OF SOCIETY WE HAVE CREATED. They are as easy, normal and unforced an expression of the American Standard of Living as electric iceboxes. We do not dream of a world in which atomic fission will be "harnessed to constructive ends." The new energy will be at the service of the rulers; it will change their strength but not their aims. The underlying population should regard this new source of energy with

68

lively interest—the interest of victims. (4) THOSE WHO WIELD SUCH DESTRUCTIVE POWER ARE OUTCASTS FROM HUMANITY. They may be gods, they may be brutes, but they are not men. (5) WE MUST "GET" THE MODERN NATIONAL STATE BEFORE IT "GETS" US. The crazy and murderous nature of the kind of society we have created is underlined by the atomic bomb. Every individual who wants to save his humanity—and indeed his skin—had better begin thinking "dangerous thoughts" about sabotage, resistance, rebellion, and the fraternity of all men everywhere. The mental attitude known as "negativism" is a good start.

AFTERWORD   Macdonald, like many others faced by new inventions, condemned it outright and all who had been involved in its creation. Yet had not the United States and Britain embarked on the quest for a bomb while believing that Hitler was trying to fashion one, and had Hitler succeeded, the history of the world would have been transformed. President Roosevelt, Britain's Prime Minister Churchill, and all the scientists would today be damned for their lack of foresight. [Actually, Nazi Germany never came close to building an atomic bomb, but the western leaders did not know that. In fact, the Germans had expelled or exterminated many of their best scientists.] In any case, once it was discovered that splitting an atom would release enormous amounts of energy, the discovery could not long remain secret. Scientists were well along the path to that discovery even before World War II started. Someone ultimately would have created this dangerous weapon.

The awesome mushroom cloud that accompanied an atomic explosion boiled up miles high into the sky. This one followed the bombing of Nagasaki.

Editorial from *Politics*, August 1945, p. 225.

THE DECISION TO DROP THE ATOMIC BOMB

INTRODUCTION   Hanson Baldwin was for many years the military analyst for the *New York Times*. The selection below is from his *Great Mistakes of the War*, where he criticizes the use of the bomb not as an outraged moralist like Dwight Macdonald, but as a practical observer who found the allied planners shortsighted about the war and its aftermath. Why did Baldwin oppose the use of the bomb? In using it, what did he believe was the result for the United States?

Perspective 3

The Atomic Bomb—the Penalty of Expediency

*by **Hanson W. Baldwin***

The utilization of the atomic bomb against a prostrate and defeated Japan in the closing days of the war exemplifies...the narrow, astigmatic concentration of our planners upon one goal, and one alone: victory.

Nowhere in all of Mr. Stimson's forceful and eloquent apologia for the leveling of Hiroshima and Nagasaki is there any evidence of an ulterior vision; indeed, the entire effort of his famous *Harper's* [magazine] article, reprinted and rearranged in his book, *On Active Service* is focused on proving that the bomb hastened the end of the war. But at what cost!

To accept the Stimson thesis that the atomic bomb should have been used as it was used, it is necessary first to accept the contention that the atomic bomb achieved or hastened victory, and second, and more important, that it helped to consolidate the peace or to further the political aims for which war was fought.

History can accept neither contention.

Let us examine the first. The atomic bomb was dropped in August. Long before that month started our forces were securely based in Okinawa, the Marianas and Iwo Jima; Germany had been defeated; our fleet had been cruising off the Japanese coast with impunity bombarding the shoreline; our submarines were operating in the Sea of Japan; even inter-island ferries had been attacked and sunk. Bombing, which started slowly in June, 1944, from China bases and from the Marianas in November, 1944, had been increased materially in 1945, and by August, 1945, more than 16,000 tons of bombs had ravaged Japanese cities. Food was short; mines and submarines and surface vessels and planes clamped an iron blockade around the main islands; raw materials were scarce. Blockade, bombing, and unsuccessful attempts at dispersion had reduced Japanese production capacity from 20 to 60 per cent. The enemy, in a military sense, was

B-29s were the first intercontinental airplanes. Flying nonstop from islands over a thousand miles away from Japan, they were able to demolish that nation's cities and industry using just conventional bombs. These planes were attacking Yokohama in late May 1945.

in a hopeless strategic position by the time the Potsdam demand for unconditional surrender was made on July 26.[1]

Such, then, was the situation when we wiped out Hiroshima and Nagasaki.

Need we have done it? No one can, of course, be positive, but the answer is almost certainly negative.

The invasion of Japan, which [chairman of the Joint Chiefs of Staff] Admiral [William] Leahy had opposed as too wasteful of American blood, and in any case unnecessary, was scheduled (for the southern island of Kyushu) for Nov. 1, 1945, to be followed if necessary, in the spring of 1946, by a major landing on the main island of Honshu. We dropped the two atomic bombs in early August, almost two months before our first D-Day. The decision to drop them, after the Japanese rejection of the Potsdam ultimatum, was a pretty hasty one. It followed the recommendations of Secretary Stimson and an "Interim Committee" of distinguished officials and scientists, who had found "no acceptable alternative to direct military use."

But the weakness of this statement is inherent, for none was tried and "military use" of the bomb was undertaken despite strong opposition to this course by numerous scientists and Japanese experts, including former Ambassador Joseph Grew. Not only was the Potsdam ultimatum merely a restatement of the politically impossible—

---

[1] The Potsdam Declaration, issued in the names of Truman, Churchill, and Chiang Kai-shek during the meeting in Potsdam in July 1945, called upon Japan to surrender unconditionally or suffer "prompt and utter destruction." It made no mention of the possibility that the Allies might allow the Japanese to retain their Emporer. *Eds.*

THE DECISION TO DROP THE ATOMIC BOMB

unconditional surrender—but it could hardly be construed as a direct warning of the atomic bomb and was not taken as such by anyone who did not know the bomb had been created. A technical demonstration of the bomb's power may well have been unfeasible, but certainly a far more definite warning could have been given; and it is hard to believe that a target objective in Japan with but sparse population could not have been found. The truth is we did not try; we gave no specific warning. There were almost two months before our scheduled invasion of Kyushu, in which American ingenuity could have found ways to bring home to the Japanese the impossibility of their position and the horrors of the weapon being held over them; yet we rushed to use the bomb as soon as unconditional surrender was rejected. Had we devised some demonstration or given a more specific warning than the Potsdam ultimatum, and had the Japanese still persisted in continued resistance after some weeks of our psychological offensive, we should perhaps have been justified in the bomb's use; at least, our hands would have been more clean.

Firebombing raids on Tokyo showed how a Japanese city could be destroyed even without the use of atomic weapons.

But, in fact, our only warning to a Japan already militarily defeated, and in a hopeless situation, was the Potsdam demand for unconditional surrender is-sued on July 26, when we knew Japanese surrender attempts had started. Yet when the Japanese surrender was negotiated about two weeks later, after the bomb was dropped, our un-conditional surrender de-mand was made conditional and we agreed, as Stimson had originally proposed we should do, to continuation of the Emperor upon his imperial throne.

We were, therefore, twice guilty. We dropped the bomb at a time when Japan was already negotiating for an end of the war but before those negotiations could come to fruition. We demanded unconditional surrender, then dropped the bomb and accepted conditional surrender, a sequence which indicates pretty clearly that the Japanese would have surrendered, even if the bomb had not been dropped, had the Potsdam Declaration included our promise to permit the Emperor to remain on his imperial throne.

What we now know of the condition of Japan, and of the days preceding her final surrender on Aug. 15, verifies these conclusions. It is clear, in retrospect, (and was understood by some, notably Admiral Leahy, at the time) that Japan was militarily on her last legs. Yet our intelligence estimates greatly overstated her strength....

The use of the atomic bomb...cost us dearly; we are now branded with the mark of the beast. Its use may have hastened victory—though by very little—but it has cost us in peace the pre-eminent moral position we once occupied. Japan's economic troubles are in some degree the result of unnecessary devastation. We have embarked upon Total War with a vengeance; we have done our best to make it far more total. If we do not soon reverse this trend, if we do not cast about for means to limit and control war, if we do not abandon the doctrine of expediency, of unconditional surrender, of total victory, we shall someday ourselves become the victims of our own theories and practices.

AFTERWORD   Baldwin believed the United States had acted immorally when it dropped the atomic bomb. Still, was the atomic bomb morally different from the British and American bombing of the ancient German city of Dresden in February 1945 merely to damage enemy morale? Twenty-five thousand died there and 35,000 were never accounted for. And was it worse than America's great fire raid on Tokyo on March 9, 1945, which burned out 16 square miles of the city center destroying 267,000 buildings and killing 100,000? By its might, the atomic bomb brought a new dimension to war. But did the lesson of the devastation of Hiroshima and Nagasaki cause world leaders in the years since to avoid clashes that could have lead to World War III and nuclear holocaust?

Excerpts from *Great Mistakes of the War* by Hanson W. Baldwin. Copyright © 1950 by Hanson W. Baldwin. Reprinted by permission of HarperCollins Publishers.

THE DECISION TO DROP THE ATOMIC BOMB

INTRODUCTION   Many of those who have written about the dropping of the bomb have stopped arguing about the morality of using it, but instead try to explain *why* it was used. Some have written that it was directed more at the Soviet Union than a defeated Japan. What explanation did Barton J. Bernstein, a professor of history at Stanford University, give in the excerpt from his essay that follows for the decision to use it?

Perspective 4

Why the Bomb Was Used

by *Barton J. Bernstein*

T ruman inherited the assumption that the bomb was a legitimate weapon for ending the war. No policymaker ever challenged this conception. If the combat use of the bomb deeply troubled policymakers morally or politically, they might have reconsidered their assumption and searched ardently for other alternatives. But they were generally inured to the mass killing of civilians and much preferred sacrificing the lives of Japanese civilians to sacrificing those of American soldiers. As a result, they were committed to using the bomb *as soon as possible* to end the war. "The dominant objective was victory," [Secretary of War] Stimson later explained. "If victory could be speeded by using the bomb, it should be used; if victory must be delayed in order to use the bomb, it should *not* be used. So far as [I] knew, this general view was fully shared by the President and his associates." The morality of war confirmed the dictates of policy and reinforced the legacy that Truman inherited. Bureaucratic momentum added weight to that legacy, and the relatively closed structure of decision-making served also to inhibit dissent and to ratify the dominant assumption.

Had policymakers concluded that the use of the bomb would impair Soviet-American relations and make the Soviets intransigent, they might have reconsidered their assumption. But their analysis indicated that the use of the bomb would aid, not injure, their efforts to secure concessions from the Soviets. The bomb offered a bonus....

...[P]olicymakers had come to assume that a combat demonstration would advance, not impair, the interests of peace—a position shared by [chairman of the National Defense Research Committee James B.] Conant, [J. Robert] Oppenheimer [director of Los Alamos], Arthur H. Compton, Nobel laureate and director of the Chicago Metallurgical laboratory, and Edward Teller, the physicist and future father of the hydrogen bomb. In explaining the thinking of the scientific advisory panel in recommending combat use of the bomb,

74

Oppenheimer later said that one of the two "overriding considerations…[was] the effect of our actions on the stability…of the postwar world." Some policymakers thought, Harvey H. Bundy, Stimson's assistant, wrote in 1946, "that unless the bomb were used it would be impossible to persuade the world that the saving of civilization in the future would depend on a proper international control of atomic energy." The bomb, in short, would impress the Soviets.

In addition, there was another possible advantage to using the bomb: retribution against Japan. A few days after Nagasaki, Truman hinted at this theme in a private letter justifying the combat use of the bombs:

> Nobody is more disturbed over the use of Atomic bombs than I am but I was greatly disturbed over the unwarranted attack by the Japanese on Pearl Harbor and their murder of our prisoners of war. The only language they seem to understand is the one that we have been using to bombard them. When you have to deal with a beast you have to treat him as a beast. It is most regrettable but nevertheless true.

In this letter, one can detect strains of the quest for retribution (the reference to Pearl Harbor and prisoners); and one might even find subtle strains of racism (Japan was "a beast"). The enemy was a beast and deserved to be destroyed. War, as some critics would stress, dehumanized victors and vanquished and justified inhumanity in the name of nationalism, justice, and even humanity.

In assessing the administration's failure to challenge the assumption that the bomb was a legitimate weapon to be used against Japan, we may conclude that Truman found no reason to reconsider, that it would have been difficult for him to challenge the assumption, and that the prospect of benefits also deterred reassessment. For the administration, in short, there was no reason to avoid using the bomb and many reasons making it feasible and even attractive. The bomb was used primarily to end the war *promptly* and thereby to save American lives. There were other ways to end the war, but none seem as effective, and all seemed to have greater risks. Even if Russia had not existed, the bombs would have

Robert Oppenheimer, left, oversaw the scientists at Los Alamos. General Leslie Groves was in direct charge of the entire bomb project.

75

been used in the same way. How could Truman, in the absence of overriding contrary reasons, justify not using the bombs, or even delaying their use, and thereby prolong the war and sacrifice American lives?

Some who have searched for the causes of Truman's decision to use atomic weapons have made the error of assuming that the question was ever open—that the administration ever carefully faced the question of *whether* to use the bombs. It was not a carefully weighed decision but the implementation of an assumption. The administration devoted thought to how, not whether, to use them. As Churchill later wrote, "The decision whether or not to use the atomic bomb to compel the surrender of Japan was never an issue." "Truman's decision," according to General Groves, "was one of non-interference—basically, a decision not to upset the existing plans."

> *"The decision whether or not to use the atomic bomb to compel the surrender of Japan was never an issue."*

AFTERWORD   Some critics have charged that the idea of using the atomic bomb was to allow America to dictate the shape of peace after the war. But Bernstein believes there are simpler and more logical reasons for its use. The whole purpose of building the bomb was to drop it to end the war. It was difficult, as he makes clear, for leaders to pause as the bitter war continued and ask new questions about this radically different weapon. Perhaps they should have held a careful review of their options and the meaning of their choices. But as the war dragged on and American soldiers died, they felt impelled to act. And the world was changed forever.

From "Atomic Diplomacy and the Cold War," by Barton J. Bernstein. Reprinted from THE ATOMIC BOMB: THE CRITICAL ISSUES, Barton J. Bernstein, ed., Copyright © 1976. Reprinted with permission.

INTRODUCTION   Stephen E. Ambrose is professor of history at the University of New Orleans. In the excerpt below from his book *Rise to Globalism: American Foreign Policy since 1938*, he, like Barton Bernstein in the preceding selection, attempts to explain *why* the bomb was used. What are his main reasons? How does he differ from Bernstein?

Perspective 5

The War in Asia

by Stephen E. Ambrose

At the February 1945 meetings with the Russians at Yalta, the Americans had done everything they could to get Stalin to promise to enter the Pacific War, including persuading [Chinese leader] Chiang [Kai-shek] to make concessions to the Russians on the Sino-Soviet border. Stalin agreed to come in within three months of the conclusion of hostilities in Europe—he would need that much time to shift troops from Germany to Manchuria. When in July the Big Three met again at Potsdam, the Americans remained as anxious as ever to have the Red Army help them out.

Then came [during the Potsdam conference] the successful test of the first atomic bomb. It inaugurated a new era in the world's history and in the tools of American foreign policy. No longer, or so it seemed, would the United States have to rely on mass armies, either those of their allies or their own. The atomic bomb had numerous advantages—it was cheaper than mass armies; it was politically advantageous, since by using it the government could avoid conscription; it was quicker. For the next two decades, American foreign policy would pivot on the bomb.

The Americans began to use the bomb as an instrument of diplomacy immediately. As Churchill summed up the American attitude on 23 July, "It was now no longer necessary for the Russians to come into the Japanese war; the new explosive alone was sufficient to settle the matter." Later the same day, reporting on a conversation with [U.S. Secretary of State] James Byrnes, Churchill declared, "It is quite clear that the United States do not at the present time desire Russian participation in the war against Japan." They did not because they did not want the Russians to join the occupation of Japan or to make gains at Japan's expense in the Far East. On 23 July, Stimson recorded that even [General George] Marshall, who had pushed hardest for Russian entry, "felt, as I felt sure he would, that now with our new weapon we would not need the assistance of the Russians to conquer Japan."

At Potsdam, Truman casually informed Stalin that the United States had a "new weapon" and was pleased when the Soviet leader did not press him for details. The Big Three then agreed to retain the Emperor after Japanese surrender, but refused to let the Japanese know this. Instead, they issued the Potsdam Declaration, calling again for unconditional surrender on pain of great destruction. The Japanese rejected the demand as it contained no guarantee on the Emperor, and Truman gave the order to drop the bomb as soon as one was ready.

What was the great hurry? This question has bothered nearly everyone who has examined the controversy raging around the decision to use the bomb. The importance of the question stems from three related factors: (1) the United States had no major operations planned before 1 November, so it had time to wait and see what the effect of the anticipated Russian declaration of war would be, or to see if the Japanese peace-feelers were serious; (2) the bomb was not used against a military target, so it did not change the military situation; (3) the Americans expected the Russians to enter the war on

Leaders of the Big Three nations—Churchill, Truman, and Stalin—met at Potsdam, Germany, in 1945 to discuss postwar arrangements in Europe.

or about 8 August; they dropped the bomb on 6 August. When the Japanese did not surrender immediately, a second bomb fell on 9 August. The British physicist P.M.S. Blackett, and later others, charged that the sequence of events conclusively demonstrated that the use of the bomb was "the first major operation of the cold diplomatic war with Russia." Its purpose was to keep Russia out of the Far Eastern settlement and had nothing at all to do with saving American lives.

78

A parallel interpretation claims that the intention was to impress the Russians with the power of the bomb and to make it clear that the United States would not hesitate to use it. America had already deployed the bulk of her troops out of Western Europe, as had the British, so the Red Army in East Europe was by August of 1945 the most powerful force in all of Europe. To those concerned about a possible Russian advance across the Elbe, the bomb seemed a perfect deterrent.

These interpretations are not necessarily wrong; they are just too limited. It is true that the death of Roosevelt allowed anti-Soviet sentiment to bubble up in Washington, especially in the State Department, but it is not at all clear that the anti-Soviet advisers were controlling events. In any case, if the motive was to keep the Russians out of the Far Eastern settlement, the Americans could have done that by negotiating a surrender in July and probably earlier, long before the Soviets were ready to declare war.

Nearly every individual who participated in the decision to use the bomb had his own motive. Some were concerned with the kamikazes, others wanted to punish the Japanese for Pearl Harbor, while there were those who thought the actual use of the bombs was the only way to justify to Congress and the people the expenditure of $2 billion on a secret project.

Life came cheap in the world of 1945. The Anglo-Americans at Dresden had slaughtered thousands and thousands of women and children in air raids that had no discernible military purpose. To kill a few more "Japs" seemed natural enough, and the racial factor in the decision cannot be ignored.

The simplest explanation is perhaps the most convincing. The bomb was there. No one in the government seriously thought about not using it. To drop it as soon as it was ready seemed natural enough. As Truman later put it, "The final decision of where and when to use the atomic bomb was up to me. Let there be no mistake about it. I regarded the bomb as a military weapon and never had any doubt that it should be used." Still, he was aware of the indirect dividends. On 9 August the Russians declared war on Japan; Truman records that "this move did not surprise us. Our dropping of the atomic bomb on Japan had forced Russia to reconsider her position in the Far East."

Unfortunately, the first bomb on Hiroshima did not bring an immediate Japanese response. The Russians, meanwhile, rolled forward in Manchuria and Southern Sakhalin. The Japanese Manchurian army surrendered. In order to prod the Japanese, the

THE DECISION TO DROP THE ATOMIC BOMB

This picture shows the B-29 Enola Gay *back at its base on Tinian island after it had dropped the atomic bomb on Hiroshima.*

United States dropped a second bomb, on Nagasaki, which insured that the Japanese government would surrender to the Americans. Even after the second bomb, however, the Japanese insisted on some guarantee about the Emperor. The Americans decided they would have to take what they could get, made the required promises, and got the surrender.

American troops occupied Japan, excluding the Russians, not to mention the Australians and British. Even though [General Douglas] MacArthur, who headed the occupation, was supposed to be a Supreme Allied Commander responsible to all the governments which had been at war with Japan, in fact he ran affairs as he saw fit, checking his decisions only with the United States government.

AFTERWORD   While most observers would agree with Ambrose that different individuals had different motives for using the bomb, it is possible to argue with him on certain points. He states, for example, that Hiroshima and Nagasaki were not military targets. But what does he mean by that? Hiroshima was an important army depot and port while Nagasaki was also a port and ship-building center. The Japanese Second Army was stationed in Hiroshima and that unit was incinerated by the bomb. As one observer remarked, this was like the United States losing the entire marine corps in an instant.

There also seems to be some confusion in Ambrose's interpretation. Since he believes the United States could have ended the war in Asia before the Soviets ever entered, why does he tie the Soviet advance in Manchuria and the Sakhalins to the quick dropping of the second bomb? The Soviet advance and the bombing of Nagasaki occurred on the same day and one event seems to have had nothing to do with the other. It might, in fact, better be argued that the Soviets entered the Asian war more quickly *because* of the bombing of Hiroshima—to be sure of getting all they could in the Far East before the war ended and perhaps even securing a share in the occupation of Japan.

From RISE TO GLOBALISM: AMERICAN FOREIGN POLICY SINCE 1938 by Stephen E. Ambrose. Copyright © 1971 by Stephen E. Ambrose. Used by permission of the publisher, Dutton, an imprint of New American Library, a division of Penguin Books USA Inc..

THE DECISION TO DROP THE ATOMIC BOMB

IS THE PRESIDENT IMPERIAL?

FROM THE EDITORS

An Imperial President—the very phrase conjures up frightening possibilities. This threat was detailed most persuasively in 1973 by Pulitzer prize-winning historian Arthur M. Schlesinger, Jr., who believed that the increase of the President's power in foreign affairs, especially during the Vietnam War, had defied the Constitution and endangered our democracy.

Fear of the President

Misgivings about the Presidency are not new in American history. Many Anti-Federalists opposed ratifying the Constitution because of what they considered to be the position's extraordinary power. The President, they warned, could "easily become king."

Still, through much of United States history, Presidents have often seemed weak—though suspicions about the office never disappeared. Perhaps more than any of his predecessors, Franklin D. Roosevelt brought the doubts about presidential power back to life. As a consummate politician and skillful war leader he dominated national politics for

From the Oval Office in the west wing of the White House, the President of the United States can exercise vast—some even call it imperial—power.

twelve years. To make sure there would never be another FDR, the Republicans, when they finally regained control of Congress in 1947, passed the Twenty-second Amendment. By limiting a President to two terms the amendment immediately decreased the chief executive's power. Since the President becomes a "lame duck" unable to seek reelection as soon as he (or, no doubt one day, she) is elected to a second term, members of Congress have less reason to fear and court him. Every President since has thought it an unwise amendment to the Constitution.

The apprehension that the Presidency was truly becoming "Imperial" came to a head during the Vietnam War. But the Constitution plainly states that only Congress has the right to declare war. The Constitution also says that the President is Commander in Chief of the army and navy. Yet what does that mean? For a long time after the adoption of the Constitution, it was understood that Commander in Chief merely meant that the President had final authority over the military—sort of the top general. It was never thought that it meant the President could commit American troops to lengthy combat overseas without the consent of Congress.

The Presidency and the Cold War

The cold war transformed the way Presidents viewed their rights as Commander in Chief. Presidents from Harry Truman on said that they had to be able to move swiftly to counter Communist aggression. They could not take the time to consult Congress, and furthermore, with their authority as Commander in Chief they did not need to.

At first most members of Congress did not complain too loudly about this expansion of the President's powers. Many historians felt that Congress's neutrality legislation in the 1930s had hindered the President's ability to take necessary actions when world war came. That unfortunate precedent made the House and Senate hesitant to intrude as Presidents claimed ever greater control over foreign affairs.

Vietnam changed Congress's thinking. Lyndon Johnson—always political—did ask Congress for the ambiguously worded Tonkin Gulf resolution allowing him to commit American forces to combat in Vietnam. But Johnson did not believe he needed the resolution. He just felt it might later keep Congress from criticizing his actions.

When Congress repealed the Tonkin Gulf resolution in 1971, Richard Nixon did not even care. His administration had already stated it was superfluous. After ordering American troops into Cambodia in 1970, President Nixon bluntly proclaimed this expansive view of his authority:

84

"I shall meet my responsibility as Commander in Chief of our Armed Forces to take the action necessary to defend the security of our American men." Congress had no role to play.

Congress Asserts Itself

Arthur M. Schlesinger, Jr., thought Nixon was even trying to bring the Imperial Presidency into the domestic scene. Watergate and Nixon's resignation, however, thwarted this attempt. But Nixon's effort, along with the Vietnam experience, awakened Congress to the need to rein in the President and exercise its own powers more actively.

For a time, under the unelected President Gerald Ford and under Jimmy Carter, who did not seem able to work with Congress, it appeared that Congress had gone too far in exerting its own authority. Observers began to wonder if the country was still governable. Then Ronald Reagan's skillful use of the powers of his office to reach his goals revived worries over the Imperial President. Congress fought hard to retain its influence in foreign affairs, causing President Reagan to burst out: "We have got to get [to] where we can run foreign policy without a committee of 535 [Congress] telling us what we can do." But, as members of Congress pointed out, this was the way it was supposed to work under the Constitution. Democratic Senator Jeff Bingaman of New Mexico

In February 1972 Richard Nixon became the first United States President to visit China. This was one of his successes that helped him win all but one state in the election that fall.

retorted, "It's a messy process, and I can understand the frustration of the executive branch, but that's the system we've got."

The reason the Constitution required the President to consult Congress was not to handcuff the President, but to force him to take into account the opinion of the people's representatives. It could be "a messy process," but one intent of "checks and balances" is to slow actions and make sure decisions are taken that a majority of the people can approve.

Some in the Reagan administration became so angered by what they considered congressional interference that during the Iran-contra affair they tried to short-circuit the nation's laws and the Constitution.

By the President's order, mammoth C-5A transport planes carried American troops and equipment from bases in the United States and Europe to serve in Saudi Arabia.

The Continuing Debate

Despite Congress's unease, the President as Commander in Chief could still act swiftly, decisively, and without formal consultation with Congress, as the attacks on Grenada and Panama ordered by Presidents Reagan and Bush showed. When President George Bush wanted to use force against Iraq, he was persuaded to ask Congress for a resolution authorizing the action—but he, too, made it clear he did not believe it was necessary. The debate over the power of the President as Commander in Chief, it is certain, is far from resolved.

The term Imperial Presidency at first referred only to the President's actions in foreign affairs. After Nixon's abuses of his office and resignation under the threat of impeachment, it was sometimes applied more loosely to all the President's powers. But, as three of the selections that follow indicate, the President is restricted in many ways. Strong character and focused leadership are the indispensable attributes of a dominant chief executive. So under some the office can be actually weak. And when the holder of the office is strong, Congress can, if it has the will, exercise its own powers to check and balance even the most Imperial of Presidents.

INTRODUCTION   Arthur M. Schlesinger, Jr., is Albert
Schweitzer Professor of the Humanities at the City University of New
York. He served as a Special Assistant to President John F. Kennedy. The
selection below is from his book, The Imperial Presidency, published in
1973. It was written after Lyndon Johnson and Richard Nixon had
claimed and exercised great presidential power during the Vietnam War.
This excerpt is concerned with President Truman's decision not to seek a
congressional resolution approving the commitment of armed forces to
Korea. Why did Truman decide not to do so? Why does Schlesinger feel
his decision was wrong?

Perspective 1

The Presidency Ascendant: Korea

by Arthur M. Schlesinger, Jr.

T his was a fateful moment. Truman had evidently not yet fully made up his mind about the scope of presidential authority. Nor did he pretend to legal skills. But he had a most eminent lawyer at his right hand [Dean Acheson]. His Secretary of State had been law clerk for Justice Brandeis, whom Truman had known and revered as a majestic expositor of the Constitution. Acheson, moreover, had been a senior member of Washington's leading law firm and was still a daily walking companion of Justice Frankfurter. On July 3 Acheson recommended that Truman *not* ask for a resolution but instead rely on his constitutional powers as President and Commander in Chief. On the same day the State Department churned out a memorandum listing 87 instances...in which Presidents had sent American forces into combat on their own initiative. Truman, impressed by the appearance of precedent and concerned not to squander the power of his office, accepted his Secretary of State's recommendation.

The State Department argument was that "the President, as Commander in Chief of the Armed Forces of the United States, has full control over the use thereof," that there was a "traditional power of the President to use the armed forces of the United States without consulting Congress," and that this had often been done in "the broad interests of American foreign policy." In the Senate Paul H. Douglas, the much respected liberal Democrat from Illinois, amplified the defense of Truman's unilateral action. Douglas rested his case particularly on the need for swift presidential action in emergencies. "With tanks, airplanes and the atom

IS THE PRESIDENT IMPERIAL?

Dignified and dapper Dean Acheson (right) advised Truman to use his power as President and Commander in Chief to send troops to Korea.

bomb, war can become instantaneous and disaster can occur while Congress is assembling and debating." Citing the UN resolutions, he contended that the introduction of armed force to drive the invaders back to the 38th parallel "was not an act of war, but, instead, merely the exercise of police power under international sanction." (He could have added that the resolutions were pursuant to the UN Charter, a treaty ratified by the Senate and that the UN Participation Act was a statute enacted by the Congress.) Though Congress had the power to declare general war, situations calling for "the retail use of force," Douglas suggested, ought to be left to the President, as they had been left throughout American history. There might be "grave dangers" in thus giving the Presidency discretionary power to commit troops to battle, but Douglas found consolation in "the sobering and terrible responsibilities of the office of President itself" and in the fact that action grossly offensive to the national interest and public will could lead to impeachment.

The constitutional case was far from conclusive. The precedents invoked by Acheson, the State Department and Douglas were precedents for limited action to suppress pirates or to protect

88

American citizens in conditions of local disorder. They were not precedents for sustained and major war against a sovereign state. As for the United Nations resolutions, while they justified American military action under international law, they could not serve as a substitute for the congressional authorization required in national law by the Constitution.

Yet in fairness to Truman it was not at all clear at the moment of first intervention that the United States was entering the grim and protracted war eventually produced by the later decision to go beyond the 38th parallel. Truman's initial decision may well have seemed to those involved less likely to risk serious war than Roosevelt's decision nine years before—also taken without reference to Congress—to send convoys into the North Atlantic. And the appeal to emergency was powerful. Even if the attack on South Korea carried no immediate and direct threat to the United States of the sort that had justified Lincoln and the second Roosevelt in their assertions of independent presidential authority, it nonetheless did demand an extremely quick decision with great potential import for American security. Nor did Truman make his decision in royal seclusion. He consulted fully and candidly with his executive colleagues. If he told rather than asked the congressional leaders, Congress soon confirmed and, in a sense, ratified American intervention by voting military appropriations and extending selective service.

For all this, it is hard not to agree with the judgment some months later of Senator [Arthur] Vandenberg, now gravely sick in Michigan. "The President's great mistake," Vandenberg wrote, "was in not bringing his Korea decision to the immediate attention of Congress (as Wilson did at Vera Cruz[1])." Truman might even, like Wilson at Vera Cruz, have requested congressional sanction without implying any surrender of presidential power by saying that he did not wish to act in a matter of such grave consequence except in close cooperation with the Senate and House. The argument against this course would have been Acheson's, that congressional debate was not "calculated to support the shaken morale of the troops or the

---

[1] On April 21, 1914, the United States bombarded and seized Vera Cruz, Mexico, because of displeasure with Mexican President Huerta. That same day, President Woodrow Wilson asked Congress for permission to use armed force against the Mexicans to uphold America's rights and dignity. It was granted on April 22. *Eds.*

Is the President Imperial?

Harry Truman greatly expanded presidential power when, without a declaration of war or other authorization by Congress, he ordered American troops to fight the North Koreans. Over 50,000 Americans died in Korea.

unity that, for the moment, prevailed at home." But this argument was hardly persuasive. If even [Senator Robert] Taft had said he would vote for a resolution, it is hard to see who would have opposed it. The passage of a resolution would have preserved the congressional role in the decision to go to war. For that matter, a resolution would have spared troop morale and national unity, not to mention the administration itself, at least one damaging form of attack after the war became unpopular. Few wars are unpopular in their first thirty days.

Korea beguiled the American government first into an unprecedented claim for inherent presidential power to go to war and then into ill-advised resentment against those who dared bring up the constitutional issue. "The circumstances of the present crisis," an executive document sourly said in 1951, "make any debate over prerogatives and power essentially sterile, if not dangerous to the success of our foreign policy." By insisting that the presidential prerogative alone sufficed to meet the requirements of the Constitution, Truman did a good deal more than pass on his sacred trust unimpaired. He dramatically and dangerously enlarged the power of future Presidents to take the nation into major war.

AFTERWORD   Aware of the opposition Truman had faced over Korea as that war dragged on, President Eisenhower was careful in 1955 to ask Congress for a resolution empowering him to send U.S. forces into the Middle East to oppose Communist aggression. But, while he got his resolution, some senators complained that they were giving "consent without advice." Strangely, when Eisenhower did send troops into Lebanon, he did not cite this resolution but insisted on his presidential prerogative, just as Truman had. Truman's precedent was snowballing.

From THE IMPERIAL PRESIDENCY by Arthur M. Schlesinger, Jr. Copyright © 1973 by Arthur M. Schlesinger, Jr. Reprinted by permission of Houghton Mifflin Company.

Theodore Sorensen served as President John F. Kennedy's Special Counsel. He was also his chief speechwriter both before and after Kennedy became President. The selection below is from his *Watchmen in the Night: Presidential Accountability after Watergate.* Sorensen believed that a President was limited in many ways—by the very nature of the position as created by the Constitution, by the rest of the executive branch, by the press, and by Congress and the judiciary. In the following excerpt, Sorensen concentrates on the powers of Congress. What are some of the ways he indicates that Congress can exercise power over the President?

Schlesinger was particularly concerned about the President's ability to use the military in foreign affairs. Does Sorenson think that Congress can act here, as well?

Perspective 2

The Facade of Unlimited Presidential Power

*by **Theodore C. Sorensen***

The principal limitations on presidential power intended by the authors of the Constitution are those exercised by Congress and the courts. Both institutions...must alter their overly deferential approach to the Presidency if they are to hold its power accountable. Neither...covered itself with sufficient glory early enough in Watergate to reassure us that the status quo is sufficient. Nevertheless, anyone under the misapprehension that the President has virtually unlimited powers is ignoring the very real power the other two branches hold....

Congress has the right to establish new agencies and abolish old ones in the executive branch, to withhold confirmation from the President's appointees, to confer additional powers on his subordinates or remove existing powers from them, to alter the terms of eligibility for their offices, and to protect them from removal. It can conduct investigational or educational hearings on every aspect of executive branch conduct, subpoena executive branch witnesses, cite them for perjury if they testify falsely, and cite them for contempt if they refuse to testify at all. It can reject, ignore, or amend the President's legislative and budget requests, withhold funds he needs, impose conditions he does not like, add to his budget more funds than he wants, override his vetoes, and limit the numbers and salaries of his White House aides.

It can prevent ratification of his treaties, block his use of the armed forces, and subject him to resolutions of censure and (as we

91

now know with certainty) impeachment. It can narrow the conditions under which executive privilege is claimed and the conditions upon which executive agreements are signed. It can initiate legislation and lawsuits in opposition to the President's interests. It can with difficulty but in time halt virtually any presidential activity it desires to halt.

To be sure, some of these rights have atrophied with disuse, some were bypassed by Nixon, and some should never be pushed to extremes without unusual provocation, because they could shut the government down. And to be sure, it is far easier for the two houses of Congress to deny to a President the affirmative action he seeks from them, as in JFK's case, than it is to block or undo action which the President takes or to compel action which he refuses to take, as in Nixon's case. Nevertheless, real power is there, and it is enormous power if used.

No President likes congressional power. Legend has it that Andrew Jackson selected the site of the Treasury Department building to the East of the White House to avoid looking out at the Capitol. But every White House knows the power is there. Every modern President creates a legislative liaison staff. He invites the leaders of Congress to breakfast, the committee chairmen to state dinners, the new members to tea. He offers favors and jobs for their constituents, grants and contracts for their districts, speeches and pictures for their campaigns. All that helps, but not very much.

He can veto bills, but not too many without antagonizing the nation, inducing Congress to attach key legislation to appropriations or other essential bills, and risking a governmental stalemate. He can *threaten* to veto bills, which gives him a tool for trading or modifying legislation....

The President can try to fight Congress by going to the people, and sometimes he should, but that has limited possibilities. He can try to ignore or defy congressional power, but only until stopped by the courts or by Congress itself—and that is now more likely. He can expand his power...in a real or self-manufactured emergency— but new legislation should make that more difficult. He can, if elected by an imposing majority accompanied by a landslide for his party in Congress, work his legislative will quickly and massively in the months that immediately follow. But those opportunities (as FDR and LBJ discovered) are rare and short-lived, as legislative coalitions realign themselves from issue to issue.

It is true that Nixon and to some extent Johnson worried less about congressional power than their predecessors. But this was not

because they usurped the powers of Congress as much as it was because the members of Congress failed to exercise their own powers....

No, Presidents sitting, standing, or running away do not have unlimited power and it should not be necessary to indict one to demonstrate that fact. Nor *should* their powers be unlimited. But neither in the light of these limitations do their legitimate constitutional powers, as distinct from the abuses thereof, need to be further reduced. The overwhelming proportion of Presidents since Jackson who have been foreclosed from more than one full term by public or party rejection, ill health, or death can hardly encourage future occupants of that office to assume that they are all-powerful.

They would do better to recollect, as President Kennedy did when he reflected upon the office, Shakespeare's account of the exchange

To carry out their programs, Presidents have to persuade Congress. In this 1961 speech to a joint session, Kennedy called for putting an American on the moon before 1970.

Is the President Imperial?

Control of the government's purse strings gives Congress enormous power if it chooses to use it. These Congressmen wanted to limit federal spending to one-third of the national income.

between the boastful Owen Glendower and the cynical Henry Hotspur:

Glendower: I can call spirits from the vasty deep!
Hotspur: Why, so can I, or so can any man; But will they come when you call for them?

Sometimes they do, Mr. President. But not as often as one thinks.

AFTERWORD   After Nixon's resignation, Congress exerted itself to make sure that Presidents like Johnson and Nixon had to pay more attention to the wishes of the legislature. Laws were passed to increase Congress's ability to deal on terms of greater equality with the President on such questions as the budget and to limit the executive's use of the armed forces, the CIA, and the FBI. For a time, under Presidents Ford and Carter, citizens began to wonder if the Presidents were so hamstrung that they were no longer able to lead the nation.

From WATCHMEN IN THE NIGHT: PRESIDENTIAL ACCOUNTABILITY AFTER WATERGATE by Theodore C. Sorensen. Copyright © 1975. Reprinted by permission of The MIT Press.

PERSPECTIVES

Perspective 3

The Stewardship of Jimmy Carter

*by **Theodore H. White***

S peaker of the House "Tip" O'Neill] was trying to deliver his Democratic majority to the President [Jimmy Carter], yet was unable to do so. And unable to do so because the President could not recognize his moment in history—recognize that he and the new Congress were at base allies and associates. The same emotions rebelling against the "imperial presidency" and the "insiders" of Washington had brought both him and the new Congress to power at the same time.

A few months after talking with O'Neill, I spent a weekend in Williamsburg, Virginia, early in 1980, with a handful of young congressmen who called themselves "the class of '76," those who had been elected on Democratic tickets the same year as Carter. They were concerned people, they were young, most of them between thirty and forty-five. They had come to this gathering on their own time, paying their own expenses, to think about the state of the nation and the party. They liked old Tip O'Neill, their House leader—but as they would like any well-meaning grandfather figure. Almost to a man, however, they disliked the President who had been elected with them in 1976. He did not function. His people at the White House treated congressmen as they had treated Georgia legislators. These new congressmen wanted to be included or persuaded; but the Carter staff was clumsy, or inefficient. One of the Williamsburg group, along with two other younger congressmen, had been invited to a private stroking session at the White House, at which the President lobbied them to support his medical insurance bill. "But why was he wasting his time on us for that?" asked the young Tennessean. "Didn't he know we were supporting that bill? He didn't have to persuade us on something we wanted ourselves." What irked most was that no one in the White House

95

would return their calls. Said one: "About the only good Teddy Kennedy's candidacy has done me is that now if I call the White House, maybe somebody will call me back." Nor were they happy about Kennedy; they would support the President in the campaign of 1980 rather than Kennedy; the President was a lesser hazard to their own campaigns for reelection. But the President would be no great help, either; and they would keep their distance.

There was then, at the base of it all, this misjudgment by Carter of the forces at his disposal. The younger people would go along with him, not out of loyalty, but out of conviction. They were to give him the rare victories he won: chopping down the pork-barrel projects of dams and river engineering; overhauling the civil service; supporting his environmental programs; supporting him in foreign affairs; supporting his energy program. But in the last year of his term, Carter had become the first Democratic President in almost thirty years to see two of his vetoes overridden by a Democratic Congress.

Even in foreign affairs, Carter had trouble defining his goals because of differences between his top advisers on foreign affairs, Secretary of State Cyrus Vance (left) and National Security Adviser Zbigniew Brzezinski.

Much more could have been done. "We made our mistakes in the first few months," said one of Carter's White House advisers. "We could have pushed SALT II through the Senate in the first few months by accepting the Vladivostok agreements, and gone on to a SALT III. Ford had signed on, Kissinger had signed on, Baker had signed on; the Republicans were hooked. But he couldn't see it. We could have asked for standby controls on gas prices in the original stimulus package. We didn't need them then, but we could have got them. They would have been vital when we came to the gasoline crisis of 1979."

96

Carter's natural support lay in the newly elected Democrats of the classes of '74, '76, and '78. But he lacked the skill to mobilize their support into legislation. He ended with no tax reform bill, no national health insurance, no welfare revision, no labor law legislation, no instant voter registration, no energy mobilization board, no Strategic Arms Limitation Treaty. In all these areas, he had entered to do the will of the people; and had ignored his Congress, as sinners and politicians. He had crested on the revulsion of the Congress and the media against the increasing power of the presidency, against the powers of Washington; but he could not redefine the presidency to bring Congress to partnership or meet the needs of the times. And so his major achievements were solitary achievements, the achievements of a President by executive or personal action, for which he must certainly be remembered more kindly than for his shortfall in legislation.

AFTERWORD   When Jimmy Carter was defeated for reelection by Ronald Reagan, American hostages were being held in Iran and the country seemed to many to be ungovernable. Talk of an Imperial President had ceased and now critics yearned for more strength and leadership from the White House. But with Ronald Reagan's assumption of the office, it soon became evident that the Presidency had not been greatly weakened by the fall of Richard Nixon, Congress's new assertiveness, and the brief years in office of Ford and Carter.

IS THE PRESIDENT IMPERIAL?

INTRODUCTION   George Will's incisive and acerbic comments on politics and politicians entertain (or annoy) those who read his columns in newspapers and magazines and watch him on television. Will, a devoted fan of the Chicago Cubs baseball team—a trying avocation— treated the coming 1988 election like an approaching baseball season in his book The New Season. Will saw an enormous change in the Presidency between July 1980, when Carter was still in power, and July 1981, when Reagan had taken command. Why does Will believe the Presidency is actually a weak office?   What does he mean when he compares the President to baseball manager Earl Weaver?

Perspective 4

Ronald Reagan

*by **George F. Will***

By 1987 Americans were being reminded, yet again, of this: The presidency is an inherently, meaning constitutionally, weak office. There is little a President can do on his own except sway the country and by doing so move Congress. Thus, the power of the presidency—unlike, say, the power of the office of the British Prime Minister armed with party discipline— varies substantially with the qualities of the occupant. And the power of a particular President can vary radically with swings in the public's perceptions of him.

Again, remember that Reagan's hold on the country's affection always rested to a remarkable degree on his reputation as a politician of clear principles clearly spoken. In the nineteenth century, an exasperated (and probably jealous) critic said: "Horatio Alger wrote the same novel 135 times and never lost his audience." In Reagan's long career he has demonstrated that in a democracy you build an audience by saying a few clear and convincing things 100,000 times. Clarity and consistency, important to any President, have been especially so to this one because those qualities, rather than a reputation for expertise, have formed an unusually large part of the foundation on which approval of him rests. That was jeopardized by the attempted appeasement of Iran, the average American's least favorite nation in the 1980s. It was this attempted appeasement that Senator Alan Simpson (R., Wyo.) said "causes the bar stools to spin out in my part of the country."

The best possible interpretation of the Iran debacle was that Reagan had failed to select satisfactory subordinates and then failed to superintend them adequately....

It is impossible to know the extent to which the word "Reaganite" will, by autumn, 1988, be identified, on balance, with success or failure. Presidents usually fail, and blame is apportioned between them ("no leadership"), the parties (the "decline" thereof), and "the system" (that is, the Constitution's separation of powers). But there is nothing wrong with the system that (in Alexander Hamilton's words) "energy in the Executive" won't cure. And effective presidential energy comes from ideas. Parties have lost the glue of patronage that made [political] machines possible, so they, too, need ideas. And there is nothing wrong with parties that unifying, animating ideas won't cure.

The chemistry of success in presidential politics is a volatile compound of two elements, ideas and temperaments. These elements are related in complex ways. Some temperaments are especially suited to communicating ideas, and to generating the kind of public affection that makes the public receptive to ideas.

What makes effective Presidents so rare is the fact that presidential power is a function of public affection. The power of the office varies radically—compare the presidency in July, 1980, and July, 1981. It varies with the grip the occupant of the office has on

President Reagan's ready smile along with his deft handling of the role of President brought him the support of a large majority of the American people.

Reagan's grip derived in large measure from his serene understanding that politics is like baseball, not football.

the public's affection and imagination. Reagan's grip derived in large measure from his serene understanding that politics is like baseball, not football. He conducted his high office the way Earl Weaver conducts his. When Weaver was the Aristotle of the Baltimore Orioles, he said: "This ain't a football game. We do this every day." Baseball's best teams lose about 65 times a season. It is not a game you can play with your teeth clenched.

Politics is like that. And sometime in the 1970s, Americans grew weary of a government with clenched teeth. They had had their fill of the "loneliness" and "splendid misery" and other rubbish about the presidency. Reagan has been an astonishing political force because he, like his country, has a talent for happiness.

AFTERWORD   Despite the problems of the Iran-contra affair, Ronald Reagan was not a key issue in the 1988 election campaign. If anything, George Bush was helped by his loyal service as Vice-President and he was easily elected to succeed Reagan. Though perhaps not as relaxed as his former boss, Bush had learned from Reagan and, like him, brought an unclenched-teeth style to the presidential office.

From THE NEW SEASON by George F. Will, Copyright © 1987 by G.F.W., Inc. a Maryland corporation. Reprinted by permission of SIMON & SCHUSTER, INC.

INTRODUCTION   Anthony Lewis writes a column for the New York Times. In the piece below he deals with the congressional resolution empowering President Bush to use force in the Persian Gulf. The Baker-Aziz meeting he refers to was a last-minute meeting between Secretary of State James Baker and the Iraqi foreign minister, Tariq Aziz. Why does Lewis believe Bush's answer was absurd? Why does he think the Framers put checks and balances in the Constitution?

Perspective 5

Presidential Power

*by **Anthony Lewis***

T he Congressional debate on war in the Persian Gulf paid belated respect to the constitutional system for deciding when America goes to war. It was an impressive debate. But it showed, in reality, how dominant is the power of the modern President.

President Bush had framed the question so it was extremely hard for Congress to say no. That was the effect of the decisions he took from early November on. He took them entirely on his own, without consulting Congress, much less asking its approval.

The critical decision was to increase the size of the American forces in the gulf to around 400,000 men and women, and to change its assignment from defending Saudi Arabia to taking offensive action against Iraqi forces. Mr. Bush made that decision around the end of October. He disclosed it after the Congressional election on Nov. 6.

The huge buildup of American soldiers reversed the role of time in the confrontation with Iraq. Before, Iraq had the burden of sustaining a 500,000-man occupation force in Kuwait over time as sanctions increasingly strained its resources. Now the American force was so large that it could not, practically, stay in Saudi Arabia through the sand storms of spring and the heat of summer.

Mr. Bush intensified the time factor by imposing a deadline. He persuaded the U.N. Security Council to authorize the use of military force if the Iraqis did not withdraw from Kuwait by Jan. 15. He made delay equal to an American defeat.

That was the posture in which the question of authorizing war came before Congress. Senator Sam Nunn argued that there was no vital American interest in freeing Kuwait in the next few months. But it took some political courage to stick to that position. A no vote risked looking like a vote for what the President had defined as defeat.

101

In the circumstances, it was remarkable that the vote was as close as it was in the Senate, 52 to 47 to authorize military action. If the resolution had come up in October, it would almost certainly have failed.

The episode reminds us what very great resources the President has in the competition for effective political power. On a foreign policy issue, especially, he can paint his side of a debate as the moral side, the patriotic side.

Modern communications have made the President the focus of national attention to an extent that the Framers of the Constitution could not have imagined. They feared—how innocent their fears seem now—the aggrandizement by Congress.

The President commands television time virtually as he wishes. Broadcasters seldom really challenge his view of events. The networks today are even refusing to accept paid advertising opposing a war in the Persian Gulf.

President Bush, with Secretary of Defense Dick Cheney (left) and Chairman of the Joint Chiefs of Staff General Colin Powell, ordered the build-up of American forces in Saudi Arabia in 1990 without formally consulting Congress.

Secrecy is a great Presidential ally. Mr. Bush concealed the decision in October that led us, inevitably, to the brink of war. His Defense Department has imposed rules of censorship on the press that may keep the American people from knowing the real nature of the war if it comes.

Presidentialism has come so far—we have got so used to it—that we do not even gasp at its extreme manifestations. There was a staggering example last week in Mr. Bush's press conference after the failed Baker-Aziz meeting.

A reporter asked the President whether he could order military action if Congress voted against authorizing it. Mr. Bush replied: "I still feel that I have the constitutional authority [to do so], many attorneys having so advised me."

102

The audacity of that answer—its constitutional absurdity—might have been expected to produce a reaction. It got none at all. The only thing one can hope is that any lawyers who did give such advice, presumably Bush Administration officials, will not have the nerve to talk again about respecting the intent of the Framers [of the Constitution].

None of this argues that George Bush is a bad man. He is not. But he may be wrong. That is why those who wrote our Constitution put in checks and balances. They believed that collective decisions would generally be wiser than individual ones, not least on the question of war.

The wisdom of George Bush's course will be tested soon. It may be that Saddam Hussein will give way. I hope he does. But it may also be that the President has so successfully destroyed all other options that he and we will find ourselves at war, with incalculable consequences.

AFTERWORD   The United States and its allies soon did go to war and, with amazing speed and miraculously low allied casualties, drove the invaders from Kuwait and occupied the southern part of Iraq. Still, as Saddam Hussein held on to power and brutally put down the revolts that broke out against him, causing more than two million Kurds and Shiites to flee, the results of the war did remain incalculable. Critics charged that President Bush had made war inevitable by sending so many troops to Saudi Arabia. Again bitter complaints were raised about the Imperial Presidency.

From "Presidential Power," by Anthony Lewis, January 14, 1991. Copyright © 1991 by The New York Times Company. Reprinted by permission.

Is the President Imperial?

Perspectives on

THE IMPACT OF THE CIVIL RIGHTS MOVEMENT

The first movement for black civil rights in American history followed the Civil War and was notable for the ratification of the Thirteenth, Fourteenth, and Fifteenth amendments. Then came military reconstruction, and new state constitutions drawn up with black participation that called for many social services never before provided in the South. The new governments elected by whites and blacks included many black legislators and officials.

This first Reconstruction came to an end after the disputed national election of 1876. Southern Democrats in Congress broke with their party and voted to make Rutherford B. Hayes President when the Republicans agreed to withdraw the last federal troops from the South and to allow the remaining Republican governments—in Florida, South Carolina, and Louisiana—to fall. The Democrats had already taken control in the other Southern states. Reconstruction was over. The South could now go its own way, for Northerners lacked the will to insure that black Southerners received equal treatment.

Martin Luther King, Jr., shown here (center, in dark suit) marching with his wife, Coretta Scott King (far right), was one of the most influential leaders of the modern civil rights movement.

105

More than 200,000 people took part in the march on Washington in 1963 to demand equal rights for blacks.

The return of the Democrats to political power did not mean that racial segregation immediately sprang to life. True, most schools were divided by race, but blacks and whites continued for many years to travel on trains together and to mix in public places. Over time, however, "Jim Crow" laws[1] spread to regulate the relationship between the races—requiring separate railroad cars, separate waiting rooms, separate drinking fountains, and separate toilets. And racial segregation was proclaimed in signs everywhere saying which facilities were for "white" and which for "colored."

In 1896, the Supreme Court put its qualified approval on these arrangements, in the case of Plessy v. Ferguson, when it approved segregated facilities, as long as they were "equal." But the Court never insisted on a test to find out whether the separate facilities were really equal. Soon "separate but equal" became an excuse for inferior schools, train and trolley accommodations, washrooms, parks, and everything else reserved for the race that many white Southerners viewed as inferior.

A New Civil Rights Movement

The second push for civil rights for blacks was started in 1941 by the courageous A. Philip Randolph, head of the Brotherhood of Sleeping Car Porters, an important organization in the days before air travel when railroads carried

---

[1] "Jim Crow" came from an old plantation song which included the line "every time I swing about, I jump Jim Crow," referring to a dance. In 1829 in Louisville, Kentucky, an actor wearing blackface makeup did a routine in which he "jumped Jim Crow." Soon the name was being used as a common reference to blacks. The first railroad car to be called a "Jim Crow" was on the Boston Railroad about 1840.

Americans across the country. On the verge of wartime, he threatened to hold a march on Washington to protest against racial discrimination in employment in defense industries. To head off the demonstration, President Franklin D. Roosevelt by executive order banned discrimination in defense factories and in the federal government on the basis of race, creed, color, or national origin. He also established the Fair Employment Practices Commission to carry out his order. The potential march on Washington was the start of a strong drive by black leaders and black newspapers to see that black Americans received fair treatment at home and in the military. "Here," according to one historian, "was where the modern civil rights movement began."

In 1944, the Supreme Court struck down the white primary which had barred blacks from any realistic voice in elections in the "Solid South." The Democratic party had been so strong in the Southern states that whoever won the primary was certain to be elected. So when blacks were not allowed to participate in the primary, they were effectively stripped of their right to vote.

Another milestone was passed in 1948 when Harry Truman ordered the end of segregation in the armed forces. And just six years later, the Supreme Court ruled in the far-reaching decision in *Brown v. Board of Education of Topeka, Kansas* that schools could not be segregated by race. Segregation by race, the Court ruled, was itself a form of inequality. For some historians, this decision marks the real beginning of the second Reconstruction, or civil rights movement. It was soon followed by Mrs. Rosa Parks's brave refusal to move from her bus seat, the Montgomery bus boycott, and the emergence of Martin Luther King, Jr., and other talented and dedicated black leaders. Then, with mounting speed, came sit-ins, freedom rides, marches, voter registration drives, brutal killings of civil rights workers, and a series of Civil Rights Acts. Schools were desegregated, the hateful "white" and "colored" signs disappeared, and blacks began to play a significant role in Southern politics.

The civil rights movement still faced the problems of racism in the North—racism based not on laws as in the South, but on facts. These problems of poor housing, unemployment, and lack of education, were not so easy to change by laws as was the segregation in the South.

But just as these problems began to be recognized, the nation was becoming deeply involved in the war in Vietnam. Soon college students and others who had worked for civil rights turned to demonstrating against the war, and the civil rights movement flickered out. The selections that follow suggest how much had been accomplished and how much remained to be done. Still, the example of the black civil rights movement led women, Native Americans, Hispanics, and other groups to make their own demands for equal treatment.

The Impact of the Civil Rights Movement

INTRODUCTION   C. Vann Woodward, Sterling Professor of American History at Yale University, is one of the country's most respected writers on Southern history. In the selection that follows, looking back in 1968, he observes with regret and nostalgia the end of what he calls the Second Reconstruction. The movement sputtered out because the urgent problems were no longer purely Southern and therefore not so plausibly blamed on the white folks below the Mason-Dixon line. Now the rest of the nation had reason to feel guilty. What were some of these problems? What other issues brought the movement to a standstill?

Perspective 1

What Happened to the Civil Rights Movement

*by **C. Vann Woodward***

"Everywhere you look with people in position of power and authority," observed Leslie Dunbar, a foundation executive, "they have things they regard as more important." Foreign crises to be solved, inflation to be curbed, elections to be won. Leaders of the Jewish community were worried about the anti-Semitism of Negro extremists. Negro leaders were divided among themselves, and their followers milled in confusion. White liberals and the New Left thought Vietnam was more important and choked a bit on the Black Power slogan. Labor leaders and politicians were concerned about their "image." And over the college campus the civil rights trumpet made an uncertain sound, or none at all. Lately embattled students carried new placards or returned to their books. A great stillness descended upon quarters long noted for outspoken opinions.

How long the trend of reaction would last and when the tide would turn we had no means of knowing. But we do know that we no longer live in the same moral, political, and intellectual climate to which we have accustomed ourselves in the period of ten or twelve years recently ended. And if we are realists we will no longer pretend that the movement for racial justice and Negro rights is sustained by the same foundation of moral assurance, or that it is supported any longer by the same political coalitions, the same interracial accommodations, and such harmony of purpose, commitment, and dedication as had once prevailed.

To call this a passing "phase," an interruption of a continuous movement, is to miss the historic integrity and distinctiveness of the recent period. It was a period of restitution, an effort to fulfill promises a century old, the redemption of a historic commitment. The appeal to history touched the Great Emancipator's "mystic chords of

memory" and evoked a crusading mood charged with romantic sentiment. It was in that mood that the mass marches ("black and white
together") were conducted. The objectives were clear and simple and
the struggle for fulfillment took place largely in the South, the proper
historic (and properly remote) setting for reconstructions. The last
major milestone of the crusade was the Voting Rights Act of 1965.

Even before that event, however, problems of a new and dis-
turbingly different character were demanding attention—things like
slums, housing, unemployment, deteriorating school and family,
delinquency, and riots. They were not wrapped in historic sanctions
and they were not amenable to romantic crusades and the evangelical
approach. They were tough and harsh and brutally raw. What's more,
they were national problems, not Southern, though the South faced
some of them too. As soon as this came home to the North the great
withdrawal set in. White congressmen from the Bronx and Chicago
set up cries of anguish and dismay as bitter as the familiar chorus
from South Carolina and Mississippi. Amid the clamor (North and
South together) the Civil Rights Bill of 1966 for open housing and protection of civil rights workers (combining "Northern" and
"Southern" issues) went down in crashing defeat.

How long before the country would be prepared to face up to
a Third Reconstruction—which is what a realistic solution of the

*Photographer Eugene
Richards took this picture
of a poor neighborhood in
north Philadelphia in 1986.
Similar ruined areas
disfigured many other
American cities.*

109

WE WANT BLACK POWER

The call for black power seemed mistaken to some members of the civil rights movement and helped to cause divisions in it.

new national problems really amounted to—remained to be seen. And whether much of the spent momentum and the old élan of past crusades would be marshaled and how many veteran leaders could be enlisted to get an entirely new program off the ground was problematical. The White House Conference of June, 1966, which was designed to do just these things, failed of its purpose. Whites and blacks share some of the blame. But public attention was diverted elsewhere. Foreign wars are notorious distractors of public attention—especially when people *want* to be distracted. Veterans of the Second Reconstruction and planners of a Third would do well to face up to the fact that the one is now over and the other is still struggling to be born.

AFTERWORD   C. Vann Woodward's essay was first published in January 1967, and in the years since then his hoped-for Third Reconstruction has only begun. Much remains to be done to deal with problems "like slums, housing, unemployment, deteriorating school and family, delinquency and riots." These daunting issues remain.

INTRODUCTION   In the excerpt below, Robert Weisbrot, a professor of history at Colby College in Maine, outlines what he believes were the successes—even if incomplete—of the civil rights movement. What were some of the major achievements he saw accomplished?

Perspective 2

A Record of Change

by **Robert Weisbrot**

L ike other reform movements the crusade for racial justice inevitably fell short of the utopian goals that sustained it. Still, if America's civil rights movement is judged by the distance it traveled rather than by barriers yet to be crossed, a record of substantial achievement unfolds. In communities throughout the South, "whites only" signs that had stood for generations suddenly came down from hotels, rest rooms, theaters, and other facilities. Blacks and whites seldom mingle socially at home, but they are apt to lunch together at fast-food shops that once drew blacks only for sit-ins. Integration extends equally to Southern workers, whether at diner counters or in the high-rise office buildings that now afford every Southern city a skyline.

School desegregation also quickened its pace and by the mid-1970s had become fact as well as law in over 80 percent of all Southern public schools. Swelling private school enrollments have tarnished but not substantially reversed this achievement. A privileged 5 to 10 percent of all Southern white children may find shelter from the *Brown* verdict at private academies; but the words "massive resistance" have virtually disappeared from the region's political vocabulary.

Hate groups once flourished without strong federal restraint, but the civil rights movement has curbed the Ku Klux Klan and other extremist threats. Beginning in 1964 the FBI infiltrated the Klan so thoroughly that by 1965 perhaps one in five members was an informant. During the 1980s, amid a rise in racial assaults, synagogue bombings, and armed robberies to bankroll fringe groups, the federal government mounted the largest campaign against organized subversion since World War II.... Federal action has encouraged private lawsuits, including one that bankrupted the United Klans of America. After a black teenager in Mobile, Alabama, was murdered by Klansmen and left hanging from a tree in 1981, the boy's family won a $7 million judgment. To pay damages the Klan had to cede its two-story national headquarters, near

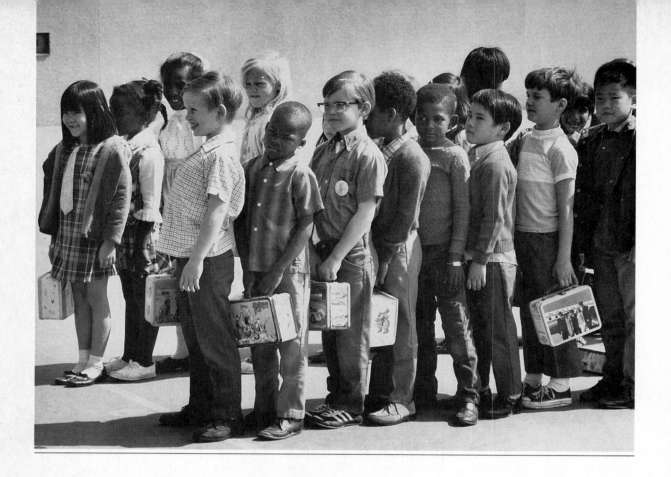

The Supreme Court's decision in Brown v. Board of Education of Topeka, Kansas *brought racial integration to many schools.*

Tuscaloosa, Alabama, to the black litigants. Reeling from legal and financial adversity, Klan membership declined from 10,000 in 1981 to less than 5,500 in 1987, the lowest since the early seventies.

Protection of voting rights represents the movement's most unalloyed success, more than doubling black voter registration, to 64 percent, in the seven states covered by the 1965 act. Winning the vote literally changed the complexion of government service in the South. When Congress passed the Voting Rights Act, barely 100 blacks held elective office in the country; by 1989 there were more than 6,800, including 24 congressmen and some 300 mayors. Over 4,400 of these officials served in the South, and nearly every Black Belt county in Alabama had a black sheriff. Mississippi experienced the most radical change, registering 74 percent of its voting-age blacks and leading the nation in the number of elected black officials (578)....

112

New currents in world affairs have reinforced the consensus to guarantee black civil rights. During the late nineteenth century Americans were largely indifferent to the nonwhite world except for the growing possibilities of colonizing or otherwise controlling it. The European nations that most influenced this country were themselves indulging in imperialism based on racial as well as national interests. Global pressures today are vastly different. Competition for the support of nonwhite nations and the near-universal ostracism of South Africa, which asserts a racist ideology, require American society to pay at least nominal homage to racial equality.

Pluralism is also more firmly rooted in American values than ever before. The black revolution stimulated others, including women, homosexuals, Hispanics, native Americans, and Asians, who frequently modeled their actions on the values and tactics popularized by Martin Luther King, Jr. Each emerging movement, while pursuing a discrete agenda, has bolstered the principle that government must guarantee equal rights and opportunities to all citizens.

AFTERWORD As Professor Weisbrot points out, even if the civil rights movement failed to achieve all its goals, its accomplishments were many. And the drive of black Americans to achieve equality stimulated other groups to push for recognition of their rights. By the 1990s, while much remained to be done, the United States had achieved the most open and equal society of any modern developed nation.

From FREEDOM BOUND: A HISTORY OF AMERICA'S CIVIL RIGHTS MOVEMENT by Robert Weisbrot. Copyright © 1990. Reprinted by permission of W. W. Norton & Company.

THE IMPACT OF THE CIVIL RIGHTS MOVEMENT

INTRODUCTION   Archibald Cox is best known as the Watergate Special Prosecutor who was fired by President Nixon. He has also been a law professor, Solicitor General of the United States, and chairman of Common Cause, a citizens' lobbying group. In the selection that follows, Cox contends that past treatment compels the use of affirmative action programs. His argument specifically relates to universities, but it might be applied equally well to other institutions, such as businesses and fire and police departments. Why does Cox think affirmative action is necessary?

Perspective 3

Affirmative Action

by Archibald Cox

Most Americans, regardless of race, color, religion, or national origin, judge "equality" in terms of the individual rather than the ethnic group. Most Americans also agree that the *ideal* of equality demands that men and women be judged on individual performance—that they be selected for opportunity, if selection is necessary, on individual accomplishment or demonstrated promise—but not on irrelevancies like race, color, national origin, or sex.

Nowhere is this ideal more important than at a university, not only because of the lessons taught by adherence to the ideal but also because adherence measures the institution's dedication to fact and reason. In an ideal world, therefore, neither race nor color would count in admission to a university. Where applications greatly outnumber available places, selection of applicants would be based on tests of promise and accomplishment, not because the tests measure a person's whole worth or even the person's future performance in a profession, but because they eliminate the irrelevant, their use teaches the ideals of equality and objectivity, and, when used with awareness of their limitations, they are the best available objective guides to future academic performance. In an ideal world, free from the practice and consequences of racial discrimination, all ethnic groups would enjoy equal opportunity on the tests.

Is this ideal equality mandated by the Fourteenth Amendment? Before answering, recall Aristotle's advice:

> In the field of moral action truth is judged by the actual facts of life, for it is in them that the decisive element lies. So we must

examine the conclusions we have reached so far by applying them to the actual facts of life; if they are in harmony with the facts, we must accept them, and if they clash, we must assume that they are mere words.

One of the actual facts of life is that an ideal, racially blind admissions program based on predictions of academic success would virtually exclude black and Mexican-American applicants from the best American professional schools. Both groups would continue to lack, perhaps for decades, any real access to higher education, the professions, and the major avenues of advancement in American life. The customary predictors of success used in admissions are often poor measures of the ultimate contribution an applicant could make to the profession and the community.... Given the actual conditions, would continued use of conventional admissions standards be the "equality" guaranteed by the Fourteenth Amendment?

The civil rights movement of the 1960s and new programs helped to integrate many colleges.

AFTERWORD The Supreme Court has had a difficult time deciding how to deal with affirmative action. Since 1981 Presidents Reagan and Bush have opposed such programs and called for a completely "color-blind, gender-neutral approach." Consequently, as their appointees have changed the character of the Court, some affirmative action programs have been struck down or their application narrowed.

THE IMPACT OF THE CIVIL RIGHTS MOVEMENT

INTRODUCTION   Thomas Sowell is a professor of economics at the University of California in Los Angeles. He is one of a number of conservative black Americans who have spoken out against affirmative action (which has also been described as "positive discrimination"). Why does Sowell believe that affirmative action actually hurts rather than helps women and minorities?

Perspective 4

The Negative Effects of Affirmative Action

by Thomas Sowell

I f the affirmative-action program was merely inane, futile, and costly, it might deserve no more attention than other government programs of the same description. But it has side effects which are negative in the short run and perhaps poisonous in the long run. While doing little or nothing to advance the position of minorities and females, it creates the impression that the hard-won *achievements* of these groups are *conferred* benefits. Especially in the case of blacks, this means *perpetuating* racism instead of allowing it to die a natural death or to fall before the march of millions of people advancing on all economic fronts in the wake of equal-opportunity laws and changing public opinion. During the 1960s—*before* affirmative action—black incomes in the United States rose at a higher rate than white incomes. So, too did the proportion of blacks in college and in skilled and professional occupations—and along with this came a faster decline in the proportion of black families below the poverty line or living in substandard housing. When people ask why blacks cannot pull themselves up the way other oppressed minorities have in the past, many white liberals and black spokesmen fall right into the trap and rush in to offer sociological explanations. But there is nothing to explain. The fact is that blacks have pulled themselves up—from further down, against stronger opposition—and show every indication of continuing to advance.

While this advance is the product of generations of struggle, it accelerated at an unprecedented pace in the 1960s, once the worst forms of discrimination had been outlawed and stigmatized. Black income as a percentage of white income reached its peak in 1970—the year *before* numerical goals and timetables. That percentage has gone down since. What affirmative action has done is to destroy the legitimacy of what had already been achieved, by making all black achievements look like questionable accomplishments, or even outright gifts. Here and there, this program has undoubtedly caused some individuals to be hired who would otherwise not have been hired—but even that is a doubtful gain in the larger context of attaining self-respect and the respect of others.

The case of women is different in many factual respects, but the principle is the same. Unfortunately, there is much fictitious "history" used to apply the "minority" concept to women. The fact is that women were a higher proportion of college faculty, Ph.D.'s, M.D.'s, people in *Who's Who,* and so forth, generations ago than they are today—and female incomes in the nation as a whole were a higher percentage of male incomes then than they are now. While many factors may have influenced their relative decline over the decades, that long decline parallels a rise in marriage rates among educated women and a rising birth rate among women in general—the population explosion—and the recent upturn for women has followed a reversal in these trends that had tied them to domesticity. In the case of women, as in the case of minorities, this all happened *before* affirmative action and its numerical goals and timetables. Their achievements were also made to look like the government's gift.

Despite criticisms of affirmative action, many people were convinced that it helped women and minorities considerably.

Who were the gainers from affirmative-action quotas? Politically, the Nixon administration, which introduced the program, gained by splitting the ethnic coalition that had elected liberal Democrats for decades. Blacks and Jews, for example, were immediately at each other's throats, after having worked together for years on civil-rights legislation and other sociopolitical goals. Whether the architects of Watergate had any such Machiavellian design in mind is a question on which each can speculate for himself. Certainly, the clearest continuing beneficiaries are the bureaucrats who acquired power, appropriations, and publicity from their activities, and who have stretched the law far beyond any congressional intent. Nothing in the Civil Rights Acts or the executive orders authorizes quotas by any name, and both the congressional debates and the specific language of the law forbid them. But the boldness of the various agencies who

THE IMPACT OF THE CIVIL RIGHTS MOVEMENT

The Supreme Court ruled in 1978 that the quotas used by the University of California at Davis Medical School to insure the admission of minority students were unconstitutional. Allen Bakke, center, had brought the case.

interpret and administer affirmative action, and the reluctance of courts to overrule administrative agencies, have permitted the growth of an administrative empire serving itself in the name of serving the disadvantaged.

AFTERWORD   Many blacks and whites disagree with Professor Sowell's view. They feel that the only way the remnants of practices and procedures that once hurt blacks can be overcome is by affirmative action. Blacks and women both question his statistics or, when they agree, what the numbers mean. Since Sowell's essay was printed in 1976, the courts have moved to rein in affirmative action programs. In 1978 in the Bakke case, the Supreme Court ruled that a numerical quota was not allowable—though a more flexible formula might be. Bakke had been denied a place in a medical school class because 16 positions out of 100 were set aside for minorities. More recently, the Court has been even more forceful. In a 1989 case, Justice Sandra Day O'Connor made it clear that the "ultimate goal" must be to eliminate race completely as a factor in "government decision making." Then, to counter the Court's decisions, Congress proposed new civil rights laws to widen affirmative action, but President Bush said these would lead to quotas and in 1990 vetoed, and as late as June 1991 threatened to veto, them.

"Affirmative Action Reconsidered" by Thomas Sowell. Reprinted with permission of the author from The Public Interest, No. 42 (Winter 1976), pp. 47–65. © 1976 by National Affairs, Inc.

INTRODUCTION   In March 1988 several reporters for *Newsweek* magazine offered a balance sheet of the successes and failures of the civil rights movement. What did they believe were some of its achievements? Why did they fear its successes actually hurt some blacks?

Perspective 5

Black and White in America

*by **David Gelman** with **Karen Springen**, **Karen Brailsford**, and **Mark Miller***

Less caring: Twenty years and a social eon have passed [since the assassination of Martin Luther King, Jr.]. Mercifully, America today is not the bitterly sundered dual society that the riot commission [National Advisory Commission on Civil Disorders, 1968] grimly foresaw. Nor is it King's promised land of racial amity. Rather, it is something uneasily between the two: a society less unequal but also less caring than it was in the '60s. There seemed, by the testimony of those who were there, more fellowship then, more ecumenical reaching out. John Lewis, who helped lead the historic Selma march for voting rights with King, recalled that not only blacks and whites joined the ranks, but rich and poor,...Protestants, Jews, Roman Catholics.... [There was a real sense of family.]

What happened to the family? Neither King, the prophet of brotherliness, nor Malcolm X, the apostle of black separatism, envisioned the icy détente that grips the two races in the '80s. Blacks and whites now more often work together, lunch together, even live side by side, yet few really count each other as friends. "It is an integrated America only to the extent that we have to come into contact with one another," says Donald Hill, a black law professor at Texas Southern University. "After 5 o'clock at night, whites and blacks retreat to their own isolated worlds."

Overall, the situation of blacks in America is still mixed, at best.... *Newsweek* has chosen to focus on blacks, rather than other minorities, because of the special relationship they have shared with whites. No other immigrant group came to America under the same circumstances as blacks, or endured such dehumanizing peonage here. As James Baldwin once wrote, "No one in the world...knows Americans better or, odd as this may sound, loves them more than the American Negro. This is because he has had to watch you, outwit you, deal with you, and bear you, and sometimes even bleed and die with you, ever since...both of us, black and white, got here—and this is a wedding."

Two changes: Two striking developments mark the black situation since the '60s. One is the emergence of an authentic black

THE IMPACT OF THE CIVIL RIGHTS MOVEMENT

Malcolm X was a riveting and eloquent speaker. At first he preached a message of hate, but a pilgrimage to Mecca persuaded him that true Muslims believed in the brotherhood of all human beings.

middle class, better educated, better paid, better housed than any group of blacks that has gone before it. As measured sometimes by white-collar occupation—anything from bank clerk to engineer—sometimes by incomes of $20,000 a year and up, the middle class grew to near 56 percent of black wage earners by 1980, according to a report by the Rand Corp., which adds, "The growth in the size of the black middle class has been so spectacular that as a group it outnumbers the black poor."

The second development is, in a way, the reverse side of the first. As comparatively well off blacks move to better neighborhoods, they have left behind a stripped-down, socially disabled nucleus of poor people who have come to be called (somewhat pejoratively) the "underclass." With a population estimated at 2.5 million—roughly three times what it was in the '70s—this group generates a disproportionate share of the social pathology usually associated with the ghetto, including high crime rates. It is the crime, especially, that keeps white—and black—fear churned up, often to the point where it obscures any more useful impulse—any beginning of interest or sympathy that might let people see each other without rancor. For many whites, the threat of violence simply justifies their native bias.

Those who have studied the underclass phenomenon up close say it is defined not so much by poverty as by certain "behaviors." Ron Mincy of the Urban Institute defines these as: people chronically on welfare, males not participating in the work force, teenagers dropping out of high school and families headed by single parents.

Devastating statistics: The isolation of the underclass was a hazard of the civil-rights movement. As it succeeded, more educated and entrepreneurial blacks moved to integrated neighborhoods, taking their gifts with them. It is an irony that distresses middle-class blacks: a deep class divide among blacks themselves. "We moved up the economic ladder and away from the old ghettos," says Roger Wilkins, a senior fellow at the Institute for Policy Studies, a Washington-based think tank.

For those left behind the statistics are devastating. Around 55 percent of the families are headed by female parents. The rate of pregnancy among 15- to 19-year-old black women is more than twice that of whites in that age group, and the infant mortality is about twice that of whites. Blacks account for about half of all crimes of violence; the rate of unemployment for black youth is more than double that of white youth. Data from a program that worked with pregnant teenagers on Chicago's West Side, says University of Chicago political scientist Gary Orfield, "showed that most of these girls didn't know anyone who had a job, anyone who went to college, anyone who was married. Within their society, it looks rational to have a baby when you're a teenage girl."

The steady economic growth that benefited many blacks gave way to economic stagnation in the mid-1970s. New plants and industries are taking root in suburban corridors, where poor blacks have little access to them. "You have to see the poverty of the urban underclass as likely to endure," says Michael Fix of the Urban Institute. "It raises the question of whether we're seeing the emergence of an American caste, a hard bottom class.... I do think that the urban underclass remains perhaps the signal issue of the next decade."

Despite the gloomy prospects at the bottom, the majority of blacks have experienced vast improvements, and their gains have become part of the social landscape. There are now close to 7,000 black elected officials—including mayors of several major cities—compared with fewer than 100 before 1955; thousands of black policemen and firefighters, where there were a conspicuous, often harassed few in the early '60s. Thousands of blacks—though scarcely enough—are in managerial jobs in major corporations. "All the jobs that were closed when I was a boy are open," says Benjamin Hooks, executive director of the NAACP. It is, nevertheless, a fragile prosperity. A portion of the new middle class is composed of women who have moved up to clerical jobs from work as domestics. Civil-service jobs account for another sizable segment.

Median black income is still only 57 percent of whites'. The black poverty rate rose to 31 percent in 1986, nearly three times that of whites, says a report by the National Urban League, which also notes "a decade-long pattern of decline" in black college enrollments, partly due to rising college costs....

121

In 1987 the National Association for the Advancement of Colored People (NAACP), headed by Benjamin Hooks (far left), formed a sports committee. Among its members were NBA Hall of Fame member Oscar Robertson (right) and, next to him, home-run king Hank Aaron.

Surprisingly, some blacks seem to accept the idea of keeping a low profile on civil-rights consciousness. Like their white counterparts, young "Buppies" are "too busy making it now," some old-line black leaders think, to contribute to the continuing civil-rights effort. Many, in fact, have come to scorn integration as a goal. Faring better economically, on the whole, they reject the notion that their well-being depends on living next door to whites. Even those who support integration seem to see it less as a moral imperative than a practical necessity. "You have to be where the opportunity is," says Vernon Jordan, the former president of the National Urban League. "Wherever white people are, there is opportunity. The system sees to that."

The whole movement has taken on that pragmatic, down-to-cases character. The arena has long since shifted to the courts,

where civil-rights lawyers carry on the battle for school busing and affirmative-action hiring practices against an often shrill opposition from local citizens.

Meanwhile there are signs of a revival of interest in the unfinished civil-rights revolution. Television, newspapers and magazines are observing the 20th anniversary of King's death with a fresh look at the problems of blacks. "The neglect of the last decade and a half has allowed the problems to fester and grow to where they've become visible again," says [Jack] Boger [of the NAACP Legal Defense and Educational Fund]. Business is also taking a new interest, he notes, as projections indicate that the labor force of the 21st century will be increasingly drawn from minorities.

Indeed, the country is nearing the day when its population will be half minorities. In some Western cities, not blacks but Hispanics have become the largest minority group. They bring with them their own profile of poverty. But it is blacks whose history has been so long and painfully intertwined with white America's.

AFTERWORD   Like the bottle that can be described either as half full or half empty, the results of the civil rights movement can be judged either by its successes or its failures. Clearly the existence of an underclass trapped in the inner cities is a major problem. Nevertheless, looking back over 50 years it is evident that significant changes for the better have taken place in the relationship between the races in the United States. Legalized racism—as evidenced in the South by the old "white" and "colored" signs, the segregated schools, buses, waiting rooms, toilets, parks, swimming pools, and water fountains—is now past history.

123

Perspectives on

WHY WERE WE IN VIETNAM?

FROM THE EDITORS

Why was the United States in Vietnam? Once there seemed a simple answer to that question. We were there to stop aggression and the spread of communism. But the longer we were involved in the area the French called Indochina (Cambodia, Laos, and Vietnam), the more difficult it became for the American people to accept that answer. The reason why we were mired in a war half a world away in the small country of Vietnam became harder and harder to explain.

The First Indochina War

When the United States began active aid to the French in Indochina in 1950, all Eastern Europe had fallen under Soviet domination, China had just been "lost" to Mao Zedong and his Communist followers, and the victorious Chinese Communists were beginning to transfer large amounts of military equipment to the Viet Minh (an abbreviated name for the Vietnamese Independence League, which was dominated by the

To offset the abstract beauty of the Vietnam War Memorial's wall of names, a realistic statue of American warriors was added.

As the war in Vietnam dragged on, protests against it grew. With the Washington monument in the background, this group of women made their feelings known.

Communists). Communist North Korea invaded South Korea in mid-1950, and only a few days later the United States sent its first military aid to the French in Indochina.

The First Indochina War—the battle between the French and the Viet Minh—came to an end in 1954 with the division of Vietnam at the 17th parallel. The Viet Minh were in the north, and the French and those Vietnamese who feared the Communists (as well as many Viet Minh followers) were in the south. Soon the French, distracted by another challenge to their empire in Algeria, were gone and the South Vietnamese were left alone. With the support of a few hundred American advisers, the South Vietnamese had to try to create a nation.

Stepping In to Prevent Communist Victory

At this point, the United States, it seemed, had the power to prevent the Communists from toppling the government of South Vietnam. Was it not our duty, as leader of the free world, to stand firm against the spread of communism?

But many wise Americans asked, was this the time and was Vietnam the place? Each Southeast Asian nation was different. To call these nations "dominoes" was simple-minded. The fall of one would not necessarily cause the fall of others. But few politicians during the 1950s, '60s, and even the '70s were willing to take the risk of being blamed for the "loss" of even one nation to the Communists. They knew only too well how Senator Joseph R. McCarthy and others had used the charge of being "soft" on communism to hound patriotic Americans from office.

In Vietnam, unlike Korea, the problem was not a simple invasion by Communists. In South Vietnam nationalists and Communists had joined in the National Liberation Front to drive out the Americans, to overthrow the government in power, and create their own government. During the war in South Vietnam, many Americans who wanted us to stay out of that country argued that the National Liberation Front was a truly independent group. The NLF, they said, only became dependent on North Vietnam as the Americans intervened. But in fact the NLF was always controlled by the North Vietnamese. When the war finally ended

PERSPECTIVES

in 1975, the North Vietnamese took over the government in the south and excluded South Vietnamese.

As the war dragged on and United States forces made little headway, the American explanations of our presence in Vietnam changed. The government told Americans that we were there to keep the "dominoes" from falling and stop aggression. We had to stay to prove we were the brave enemies of communism, and "to avoid humiliation." The war came to seem not only a fight against communism in Vietnam but against all international communism. Now it was also an effort to "contain" Communist China. But these reasons blindly ignored conditions inside Vietnam.

Ending U.S. Involvement

After years of a costly, bloody, and unsuccessful struggle, it became clear that there was not the will in the United States to continue the war. But the more American lives were lost, the harder it was to find a way to get out that would not dishonor the patriotic dead and disgrace the United States. Finally, President Nixon gave up the quest for victory, and sought only "peace with honor." He began in 1969 to turn the fighting over to the South Vietnamese and bring American troops home. Though the war would drag on for four more years, the United States was only trying not to be humiliated. For as President Nixon put it, we did not want to appear a "pitiful, helpless giant."

The United States had little to gain by bleeding in Vietnam. There were no riches to be seized, no natural resources to be taken, no strategic positions that could not be replaced. We were there, as the U.S. government honestly said, to protect the South Vietnamese. To some observers, even some who once opposed the war, the later history of Indochina proved that the United States was right to be there. But others hold that the massive intrusion of the United States was a tragedy for the entire area and especially for the people of Cambodia.

What the United States accomplished in Indochina and the "lessons" of our involvement in Vietnam will long be debated. The authors of the following selections introduce us to some of the most interesting unanswered questions.

INTRODUCTION   Bernard Fall was a French citizen who fought in the Resistance against the Nazis during World War II. He was the author of several books on Vietnam and was killed there in 1967 while on a research trip. At the time of his death he was Professor of International Relations at Howard University in Washington, D.C. This selection, which is from *The Two Viet-Nams*, was written in 1967, shortly before Fall's death.

The Geneva peace conference of 1954, which brought the first Indochina war to an end, called for elections to be held in July of 1956 in Vietnam to vote on unification. Neither the United States nor South Vietnam had agreed to the elections. Fall argues that it is not surprising that South Vietnam refused to participate in elections (the plebiscite he refers to). But he thinks that since President Ngo Dinh Diem of South Vietnam rejected elections, he needed to take immediate action to prevent war. What actions does Fall think Diem should have taken, and why does he think Diem failed to act? Finally, how does Fall think that Diem's conduct was an important factor in producing the Second Indochina War?

Perspective 1

The Second Indochina War: The Reason Why

by Bernard B. Fall

The historical record will show that, unfortunately, the single offender most responsible for precipitating the Second Indochina War was the Ngo Dinh Diem regime itself. It was fully understandable in 1956 that South Viet-Nam (with a population of about 13 million, as against the North's 15 million) did not relish the idea of a plebiscite [elections on unifying Vietnam]...—that surely would have sealed its fate. But it was *precisely* that refusal which should have incited it to a maximum effort at creating with its northern neighbor..."a state of tolerable coexistence"! That is exactly what the two Germanies did, with their $500 million-a-year trade, regardless of the Berlin Wall or of promises going back as far as Tehran or Yalta for a reunified Germany.

On that account, the historical record is brutally clear. Once Hanoi accepted the fact of a permanent division (some writers...affirm that it had already accepted that fact at Geneva in 1954), it set about creating *de facto* conditions to make the division tolerable. This was not simply a matter of basic goodness for the North Vietnamese; but, more than ever before, they needed South Vietnamese rice and they hoped to sell such cash items as

128

coal and cement. The machinery for [cooperation between the two Viet-Nams]...existed, and in fact, one such agreement...[dealing with mail between the two countries] was signed by authorities of both regimes at Haiphong, in North Viet-Nam. Had Ngo Dinh Diem (and, presumably, his American advisers) believed in making South-North relations tolerable, such agreements, as in the German case, could soon have covered the whole gamut of economics, cultural relations, and even limited travel.

North Viet-Nam repeatedly tried to achieve this, by letters from Prime Minister Pham Van Dong to Diem...particularly on December 22, 1958. [This]...letter was of key importance because it spelled out a four-point program that, with the proper safeguards, could have become...an ideal normalization program between the two Viet-Nams.... It did not commit Saigon to anything over which it had no control or which it (or Hanoi, for that matter) could not stop at will.

Diem did not even bother to reply to the letter. If anything, its reasonableness persuaded him (and whom else?) that Hanoi was in the throes of a severe crisis that South Vietnamese intransigence [refusal to cooperate] would bring to a rapid eruption.... It was only this consistent rejection of normalization overtures, plus the gradual disintegration of the Diem regime under revolutionary pressures from *both* sides—after all, its own army tried to overthrow it three times, and finally did—which provided North Viet-Nam with an almost irresistible rationale for participating in the widening insurgency.

The oversimplified theory that the whole Viet-Nam problem started with a single-minded decision by Hanoi to commit aggression

Vietnamese President Ngo Dinh Diem, shown here in the presidential palace in Saigon, was overthrown and murdered in November 1963.

129

In 1962 there were some 10,000 American advisers in Vietnam helping to train South Vietnamese troops.

completely fails to explain why a country that did not even engage in the low-risk attempt at winning the South through political pressure in 1956 would, a bare year or two later, decide to conquer it militarily at the far higher risk of a military collision with the United States, or even of a world war.

But after all, the Second Indochina War is neither the first nor the last war in history to be fought over an erroneous [false] assumption or a total failure of diplomacy.

AFTERWORD   Diem was overthrown and murdered during a military coup in 1963. The United States, which had lost confidence in his leadership, was not displeased. At that point, there were 16,000 American military advisers in Vietnam and, though few realized it, the United States was deep in a quagmire which would consume ten years and thousands of American lives.

From pages 336–337 of *The Two Viet-nams: A Political and Military Analysis* by Bernard B. Fall. Copyright © 1967. Reprinted with permission.

INTRODUCTION   As a reporter for the *Baltimore Sun*, Arnold Isaacs served in Vietnam from 1972 to 1975. He left Saigon by helicopter shortly before the North Vietnamese tanks rolled in. He retired as a journalist in 1978 to write *Without Honor: Defeat in Vietnam and Cambodia*, the book from which this brief excerpt is taken.

Isaacs examines the effort by the American military to "win" the war, and places blame for the apparent lack of American success on the battlefield. Why, he asks, didn't the American army—possessing the greatest firepower of any army ever known—defeat the poorly equipped North Vietnamese?

Perspective 2

The Americans Leave

by Arnold R. Isaacs

The United States was not beaten: that was, and has remained, an article of faith for most American military professionals.

In the narrow sense that major U.S. units were never overwhelmed in battle, it is true. Yet on that day in March of 1973 [the day the last U.S. troops left Vietnam], if you looked on military order-of-battle maps for the place names that had appeared in America's newspaper headlines or flashed across its television screens, you would find nearly all of them in Communist-held zones. The Ia Drang valley, Dak To, Con Thien, Khe Sanh, the Parrot's Beak, the nameless ridge somebody called Hamburger Hill—not one of them remained in friendly hands. U.S. commanders never stopped explaining that the war was not fought to hold territory. But to a confused and increasingly skeptical public at home and to many of the soldiers themselves, the pattern of bloody battles followed by abandonment of the battlefields came to symbolize the futility of an ill-conceived war. "UUUU," some GIs scrawled on their helmet covers, standing for "the unwilling, led by the unqualified, doing the unnecessary for the ungrateful."

Those soldiers and their comrades fought bravely, on the whole, if often cynically. They surely deserved better than the indifference or contempt many of them met when they returned home; whoever was to blame for the war's mistakes, it was certainly not the young men who were sent to fight it.

It was also true, though, that what was achieved by American arms hardly seemed commensurate with [equal to] the effort that had been made or the resources that had been expended—which

131

Army chief of staff General William Westmoreland, shown here in 1970 inspecting members of the 101st Airborne Division, commanded U.S. forces in Vietnam from 1965 to 1968.

were vastly greater than those available to the enemy. The American expeditionary force in Vietnam, said one army study, enjoyed "a degree of tactical mobility and devastating conventional firepower unparalleled in military history." In contrast to past wars, commanders were not subject to rationing of weapons, ammunition, or fuel. Whatever they said they needed, in most cases, they got....

The American army and its supplies were flown about in more than 3,000 helicopters. It was supported by hundreds of fighters and bombers. It had every manner of military gadgetry, it seemed, ever devised by man. It was facing an opponent, as the former pacification chief Robert Komer once wrote, "that walked, that used mortars as its chief form of artillery, that used almost no armor [tanks, etc.] until 1972, and that was near-totally lacking in air support." Yet what was achieved was no better than an ambiguous standoff.

Many, perhaps most, military men blamed political limitations for the war's disappointing result. But there was another view: that U.S. military commanders massively misunderstood and mismanaged the conflict.... The Americans had no strategy except to inflict casualties they hoped would break the Communists' will to continue the war. They did kill appalling numbers, but their calculus proved incorrect; throughout the war, the Communists proved able to absorb their losses without either altering their long-range objective or losing discipline in their army or population.

In their helicopters, American and South Vietnamese troops could move easily over the jungles of Vietnam, but superiority in the air did not guarantee American success.

AFTERWORD   How hard it was to defeat the Viet Cong and North Vietnamese was revealed by their Tet offensive. They suffered massive losses in the attack—perhaps 50,000 of their soldiers died, compared to 10,000 lost by the United States and South Vietnam—but the United States seemed no closer to victory. In fact, General William Westmoreland, when he asked for more American troops, said: "A setback is fully possible if I am not reinforced."

From pages 125–127 of *Without Honor: Defeat in Vietnam and Cambodia* by Arnold R. Isaacs. Copyright © 1983. Reprinted by permission of The Johns Hopkins University Press.

WHY WERE WE IN VIETNAM?

INTRODUCTION   Stanley Karnow is a journalist who reported on Vietnam first from France in the 1950s and then from eastern Asia into the 1980s. He is the author of *Vietnam, A History* (New York: The Viking Press, 1983), an account of the war. Karnow returned to Vietnam in 1990, and during his visit he interviewed General Vo Nguyen Giap, the man who had built and commanded the North Vietnamese army.

General Giap indicates how difficult it would have been to defeat the Vietnamese Communists. What reasons does Giap give for why the North Vietnamese were fighting and what they were willing to sacrifice to achieve their goals?

Perspective 3

Giap Remembers

by Stanley Karnow

H ere was General Vo Nguyen Giap, the Vietnamese Communist commander, the peer of Grant, Lee, Rommel, and MacArthur in the pantheon of military leaders.

A bold strategist, skilled logician and tireless organizer, Giap fought for more than 30 years, building a handful of ragtag guerrillas into one of the world's most effective armies. He surmounted stupendous odds to crush the French, but his crowning achievement was to vanquish America's overwhelmingly superior forces in Vietnam—the only defeat the United States has sustained in its history....

[A]s he began to talk seriously, he exploded in a torrent of words. Endowed with a prodigious memory, he recalled the names of old comrades or detailed events dating back decades.... He admitted that, yes, "there were difficult moments when we wondered how we could go on." Yet, he thundered, "We were never pessimistic. Never! Never! Never!"

Giap's men did indeed show phenomenal tenacity during the war, confounding United States strategists who assumed that sheer might would crack their morale. [General William] Westmoreland, pointing to the grim "body count" of enemy dead, constantly claimed that the Communists were about to collapse. Following the war, still perplexed by his failure, Westmoreland said, "Any American commander who took the same vast losses as Giap would have been sacked overnight."

But Giap was not an American among strange people in a faraway land. His troops and their civilian supporters were fighting on their own soil, convinced that their sacrifices would erode the patience of their foes and, over time, bring Vietnam under Communist control.

134

The puckish face of Vietnamese Communist army commander General Vo Nguyen Giap did not reveal his iron determination.

He had used this strategy against France, and he was confident that it would work against the United States.

"We were not strong enough to drive out a half-million American troops, but that wasn't our aim," he told me. "Our intention was to break the will of the American Government to continue the war. Westmoreland was wrong to expect that his superior firepower would grind us down. If we had focused on the balance of forces, we would have been defeated in two hours. We were waging a people's war— *a la manière vietnamienne* [in the Vietnamese way]. America's sophisticated arms, electronic devices and all the rest were to no avail in the end. In war there are the two factors—human beings and weapons. Ultimately, though, human beings are the decisive factor. Human beings! Human beings!"

How long was he prepared to fight? "Another twenty years, even a hundred years, as long as it took to win, regardless of cost," Giap replied instantly. What, in fact, had been the cost? "We still don't know," he said, refusing, despite my persistence, to hazard a guess. But one of his aides confided to me that at least a million of their troops perished, the majority of them in the American war. As for the civilian toll, he said, "We haven't the faintest idea."

135

WHY WERE WE IN VIETNAM?

Despite its technological superiority, the United States was unable to defeat the North Vietnamese and Viet Cong.

Listening to these horrendous statistics recalled to me the Americans who observed during the war that Asians have little regard for human life. But, judging from the carnage of two World Wars, the West is hardly a model of compassion. Moreover, Giap maintains, the Communists would have paid any price for victory because they were dedicated to a cause that reflects Vietnam's national heritage—a legacy that has also fueled its fierce martial spirit.

"Throughout our history," he intoned, "our profoundest ideology, the pervasive feeling of our people, has been patriotism." I knew what he meant. A battlefield for 4,000 years, Vietnam is awash in stories of real or mythical warriors who resisted foreign invaders, mainly Chinese. Its struggles forged a sense of national identity that is still alive in poetry and folk art, and in rural pagodas where children burn joss sticks before the statues of fabled heroes and heroines....

He gripped my hand as we parted, saying: "Remember, I am a general who fought for peace. I wanted peace—but not peace at any price." With that he walked off briskly, leaving me to contemplate the cemeteries, the war monuments and the unhealed memories in France, America and Vietnam, and the terrible price their peoples paid.

AFTERWORD   Despite their heavy losses of soldiers and civilians during the long years of war, the Vietnamese survived. Though the country's economy was destroyed and many of its people fled, the population has continued to grow. Doubling its numbers from 1955, by 1988 the country counted some 59 million people. The old Communist leaders in Hanoi had successfully conquered South Vietnam, but they have yet to bring prosperity to their growing population.

From "Giap Remembers," by Stanley Karnow, June 24, 1990. Copyright © 1990 by The New York Times Company. Reprinted by permission.

Richard J. Barnet, the author of the selection below, is a specialist in international politics. A founder of the Institute for Policy Studies in Washington, D.C., he has served as its co-director, and since 1977 he has been a senior fellow.

This excerpt by Barnet was written in 1968 during the height of the war. He described two possible approaches to the problem in Vietnam—political and military. What approach did he believe the United States was taking, and what did he predict would be the consequences of this choice?

Perspective 4

America in Vietnam

*by **Richard J. Barnet***

T he means that a large power selects to intervene in a small one's affairs determines the political complexion of the client country. Having decided to characterize the problem of Vietnam as primarily military and to defer political repair until "victory," the United States had little choice but to promote and support those politicians who were dedicated only to military resistance. Despite continued talk about "pacification" and, later, "constitutional reform" and other efforts to attack the political causes of insurgency, these approaches received less and less attention as the military program shifted into high gear.

By 1967 it was largely an American war fought with a rain of bombs at a rate that exceeded the monthly tonnage of bombs dropped on Nazi Germany at the height of World War II. Despite five hundred thousand men and more, mastery of the air over South Vietnam, and increasing bombardment of strategic and economic targets in North Vietnam, the war was not going well for the United States. The Vietcong continued to recruit more men. They returned to villages once "cleared" by costly and bloody "search-and-kill" operations. The South Vietnamese army played less and less of a role. Little progress had been made on building a political basis for the restoration of peace. Much of the South Vietnamese population, to the confusion and fury of their American protectors, continued to cooperate with the Vietcong and refused to warn the Americans when guerrilla attacks were coming. As the casualties mounted, Vietnamese and American,

These North Vietnamese women, camouflaged for concealment and equipped with old rifles, were ready if needed to fight for their country.

the escalation made more evident than ever the political and moral bankruptcy of one country using military force to stop a political movement in another.

AFTERWORD   Barnet did not doubt that the problem in South Vietnam was political and not military. Yet, instead of concentrating on the need to build stronger political institutions and greater popular support, the American response was more troops, more arms and equipment, more bombs. As a result, he believed the South Vietnamese government became alienated from its citizens, dependent on the United States, and increasingly less able to survive on its own.

INTRODUCTION To mark the fifteenth anniversary of the fall of Saigon (April 30, 1975), the *Wall Street Journal* published the following statement by three Americans "whose lives were touched by the Vietnam War." These three, who had spent many of the intervening years in Asia, were: Arthur Kobler, a Foreign Service officer in Singapore; W. Gage McAfee, an international attorney in Hong Kong; and Warren Williams, a public affairs consultant in Hong Kong.

The authors look back on the war from the perspective of all Southeast Asia. They examine some basic questions about the war: Why was it fought? What were its far-reaching consequences? Was the devastation caused by the war worth it?

Perspective 5

Setting the Vietnam Record Straight

*by **Arthur Kobler**, **W. Gage McAfee**, and **Warren Williams***

L ike most Americans in their 40s and 50s, our lives were scarred by the Vietnam War. We were among those who went to Vietnam—one a diplomat, another an AID [Agency for International Development] lawyer, the third a Special Forces officer—persuaded that our national objectives in pursuing the war were fundamentally correct. Fifteen years ago, two of us worked on the Embassy evacuation in Vietnam: one left on a helicopter from the roof of the Embassy, another on the last Air Vietnam flight. The third worked on the evacuation from Tokyo. We were all shattered by the collapse of the American effort.

Whichever side one took during the war, much has happened since then that should have provoked rethinking the war experience. Yet, despite the disintegration of communism, the rise of regional powers and events that have forced us to redraw the global strategic map, the American view of Vietnam remains frozen in a time warp.

For the sake of our national peace of mind, the American people must finally come to terms with the meaning of the war. Only then will the U.S. be prepared to assess dispassionately the national interest and shape a balanced policy, motivated neither by penance nor revenge.

According to popular mythology, the U.S. fought the Vietnam War on the wrong side, and our soldiers went there to kill innocent people and smoke pot. Our pop culture—exemplified by films like "Platoon" and "Born on the Fourth of July"—panders to this distorted perception. As a result, most Americans continue to wallow

139

in guilt, bitterness and unreconciled hostility toward Vietnam. Most Americans are also astoundingly unaware of what has happened in Southeast Asia during the past 25 years.

The Vietnam War, like all wars, wreaked awful devastation. Of that, no one can be proud—Vietnamese or American. Nevertheless, the transcending legacy of the U.S. war effort is profoundly constructive: It is the growing prosperity and vitality of the 300 million people who live in Southeast Asia outside of Indochina and Burma. That compelling truth, self-evident to many in this region, including most eloquently Singapore Prime Minister Lee Kuan Yew, still seems lost on the majority of Americans.

Too few of us recall how tenuous this region's equilibrium was in the early 1960s. Virtually every country was beset by a virulent Communist movement that threatened stability and development: Thailand, Malaysia, Singapore, Indonesia, the Philippines. Today, Southeast Asia is the fastest growing region in the world, and one of immense importance to our own economy and national security. There are surely many reasons for its remarkable success, including strong national leadership, sound policies and access to U.S. markets. But all these positive elements would have been nullified had the U.S. not made a determined stand in Vietnam and steadfastly continued to this day to guarantee the security of this vast region. Those sustained efforts eased insurgent pressure on the rest of Southeast Asia and provided breathing space to achieve stability and growth.

Danger lurked everywhere in the thick tropical vegetation of South Vietnam.

In retrospect, the unraveling of the war effort in South Vietnam in 1975 was not the conclusive event it seemed to us at the time. By 1990 it has become clear that the basic objective of U.S. policy in Indochina—safeguarding the security and promoting the prosperity of Southeast Asia—was splendidly achieved.

Moreover, yet another paradox has emerged: Communist Indochina itself is awakening to the stark reality of its own failed revolution and is slowly groping toward principles it once scorned—open markets, private property, pluralism. This awakening is surely painful and hesitant, but no less inevitable than the dramatic transformation we have witnessed in Eastern Europe.

On this 15th anniversary of the fall of Saigon, it is fitting to set the record straight, to re-examine this episode in our history—not only the grief it caused, but also its significance for Asia and for America's vital interests. This process is an essential step in restoring the dignity and honor of 55,000 American servicemen who perished in the war and of millions of Vietnamese veterans, South Vietnamese and American. History has vindicated their sacrifices.

AFTERWORD   Was it necessary to lose 55,000 American lives and countless Vietnamese to "save" the rest of Southeast Asia? Were there no alternatives? Were the other nations in the region as weak as the authors believe? These questions will long be argued. But these three authors who knew the country were convinced that the United States's presence, and the sacrifice of American lives, were required.

From "Setting the Vietnam Record Straight," by Arthur Kobler, Gage McAfee, Warren Williams. Reprinted with permission of The Wall Street Journal. © 1990 Dow Jones & Company, Inc. All rights reserved.

INTRODUCTION   Norman Podhoretz has been the editor-in-chief of *Commentary* magazine since 1960.

In the excerpt that follows he reminds readers of the "lesson of Munich." In that German city just prior to World War II, British Prime Minister Neville Chamberlain—hoping to avert war—gave in to Nazi Germany's threat of force. But instead of achieving "peace in our time," Chamberlain's appeasement brought about "the certainty of a world war." Podhoretz compares "the lessons of Vietnam" with that of Munich. He then raises the question: Are we forgetting the lesson of Munich and learning the wrong lesson from Vietnam?

Perspective 6

Why We Were in Vietnam

by **Norman Podhoretz**

Even before April 30, 1975, [when Saigon fell to the North Vietnamese army and the last American helicopter left the roof of the U.S. embassy]…Vietnam had become perhaps the most negatively charged political symbol in American history, awaiting only the literal end of American involvement to achieve its full and final diabolization [to make something devilish]. From a narrowly political point of view, it had become to the generation that had experienced it what Munich had been to an earlier generation: the self-evident symbol of a policy that must never be followed again.

Indeed, for many people whose original support of American intervention in Vietnam had been based on memories of Munich, Vietnam not only replaced it but canceled it out. To such people the lesson of Munich had been that an expansionist totalitarian power could not be stopped by giving in to its demands and that limited resistance at an early stage was the only way to avoid full-scale war later on. Prime Minister Neville Chamberlain, returning to England from the conference in Munich at which Nazi Germany's claims over Czechoslovakia had been satisfied, triumphantly declared that he was bringing with him "peace in our time." But as almost everyone would later agree, what he had actually brought with him was the certainty of a world war to come—a war that Winston Churchill, the leading critic of the policy of appeasement consummated at Munich, would later call "unnecessary." According to Churchill, if a line had been drawn against Hitler from the beginning, he would have been forced to back away, and the sequence of events that led inexorably to the outbreak of war would have been interrupted.

142

Obviously, Vietnam differed in many significant ways from Central Europe in the late 1930s. But there was one great similarity that overrode these differences in the minds of many whose understanding of such matters had been shaped by the memory of Munich. "I'm not the village idiot," Dean Rusk, who was Secretary of State first under Kennedy and then under Johnson, once exploded. "I know Hitler was an Austrian and Mao is a Chinese.... But what is common between the two situations is the phenomenon of aggression." In other words, in Vietnam now as in Central Europe then, a totalitarian political force—Nazism then, Communism now—was attempting to expand the area under its control. A relatively limited degree of resistance then would have precluded the need for massive resistance afterward. This was the lesson of Munich, and it had already been applied successfully in Western Europe in the forties and Korea in the fifties. Surely it was applicable to Vietnam as well.

When, however, it began to become evident that, in contrast to the cases of Western Europe and Korea, the differences between Vietnam now and Central Europe then were more decisive than the similarities, the relevance of Munich began to fade, and a new set of lessons—the lessons of Vietnam—began to take hold. The legacy of Munich had been a disposition, even a great readiness, to resist, by force if necessary, the expansion of totalitarianism; the legacy of Vietnam would obversely be a reluctance, even a refusal, to resist, especially if resistance required the use of force.

As South Vietnam fell to the Communists in April 1975, Americans and selected South Vietnamese friends were helicoptered to safety aboard navy ships off the coast.

AFTERWORD   Podhoretz felt that the "lesson of Munich" was not one to be forgotten. He worried that after Vietnam the United States would be afraid to stand up to aggression. But he may have breathed easier as President Bush ordered U.S. troops in August 1990 into Saudi Arabia after Iraq attacked and occupied little Kuwait and appeared ready to invade Saudi Arabia. When Iraq still failed to withdraw, American and allied forces attacked early in 1991 and swiftly defeated Iraq. When the fighting stopped, President Bush declared that we were, at last, over the Vietnam syndrome.

WHY WERE WE IN VIETNAM?

THE STRUGGLE FOR WOMEN'S RIGHTS

The movement for women's rights, like the civil rights movement, has had several stages. And the pursuit of equal treatment for women has often been spurred on by the demand for better treatment for blacks and others.

The First Women's Rights Movement

The first women's rights movement developed during the reform era before the Civil War. Banned from an abolitionist convention in England in 1840 because they were women, Elizabeth Cady Stanton and Lucretia Mott turned some of their energy to the push for women's rights. They organized a Women's Rights Convention that met at Seneca Falls, New York, on July 10, 1848, and that issued a statement modeled on the Declaration of Independence. It proclaimed that "all men and women are created equal" and called for women to be given immediately "all the rights and privileges which belong to citizens of the United States"—including the right to vote.

One hundred thousand people, most of them women, marched in Washington during July 1978 calling for an extension of the time limit on the adoption of the Equal Rights Amendment. Congress later extended the date from 1979 to 1982.

145

But many Americans disagreed. They believed that the family was the basis of society; that it was a single unit; and that allowing women to vote would break that unity. Greater freedom for women, one United States Senator predicted during a congressional debate in 1866, would put them "in an adversary position to man and convert all the now harmonious elements of society into a state of war, and make every home a hell on earth."

The first women's rights movement continued into the 1880s but was often overshadowed during the Civil War and Reconstruction by the question of the place of blacks in American society. The movement foundered in the 1870s and 1880s when some women, led by the quick-witted and outspoken Victoria Woodhull, called for free love. That was too much for many American women and the movement splintered and lost its force.

Votes for Women

In the face of vehement opposition to controversial ideas such as free love, the radical feminists retreated and the women's movement began to concentrate in the 1890s on the limited goal of women's suffrage. Women had first received the right to vote in Wyoming in 1869. But by 1896 only the western states of Utah, Colorado, and Idaho had followed. In the succeeding years, the leaders of the women's movement, now people like Jane Addams and Florence Kelley of Hull House, and the organizing genius Carrie Chapman Catt, tied the women's suffrage question to the other reform ideas of the Progressive Era.

While some feminists took to the streets to demonstrate, conspicuously at the time of Woodrow Wilson's first inaugural in 1913, their main effort went into lobbying in state legislatures and the Congress. Helped by the contributions of women to the war effort during World War I and to Wilson's war policies, their campaign succeeded in a number of states. In 1918, President Wilson wrote to Mrs. Catt, "The services of women during the supreme crisis have been of the most signal usefulness and distinction. It is high time that part of our debt should be acknowledged and paid."

As a result of their brilliant and vigorous campaign for suffrage, when the Nineteenth Amendment to the Constitution giving women the right to vote was presented to Congress in 1919, it did not seem controversial at all. It swept to an easy victory, and just fourteen months later the amendment had been ratified by the necessary two-thirds of the states.

By the time the Nineteenth Amendment was passed in 1919, many women had convinced themselves that it was the panacea that would

146

bring equality. Women, it was believed, would vote as a group and then could accomplish any change they wanted. It took time for them to realize that women were not united on all issues. But the depression of the 1930s and then World War II distracted women from their own cause and interfered with their ability to mount a new drive for equality. After those years of disruption, the decade of the 1950s was a time when home, family, and children became the cherished goals of most women.

Alice Paul, one of the leaders in the fight for women's suffrage, celebrated victory in 1920 by sewing a star on the flag of the National Women's party.

The New Feminism

It was a homemaker and writer named Betty Friedan who ignited the next stage of the women's movement. After graduating from Smith College in 1942, she married and then, like so many of her generation, concentrated on raising her three children. On the side, however, she wrote articles for women's magazines. In 1957, for the fifteenth reunion of her Smith College class, Friedan conducted a survey of her classmates. To her surprise, she discovered that many of them were dissatisfied with their lives. These revelations, along with numerous conversations with friends, and

THE STRUGGLE FOR WOMEN'S RIGHTS

In the 1950s the ideal woman was expected to spend her time at home— and among life's tragedies might be the failure of a cake.

the letters she received in response to an article she wrote called "Women Are People, Too," convinced her that women's discontent was "the problem that has no name."

Betty Friedan's epoch-making 1963 book describing women's problems, *The Feminine Mystique,* revived the women's rights movement. Once again it was aided by the demand for equal treatment for black Americans. Sensitized to injustice by the civil rights movement, Americans were readier to listen to the demands of women. The new movement had many triumphs, as you will read in the selections that follow. But those successes, and the reduced zeal for reform in the seventies and eighties, left feminists divided and unsure about their next goals.

In a report for *U.S. News & World Report* magazine in February 1990, Alvin P. Sanoff told of women's frustration and disillusionment over the achievements of the women's rights movement of the 1960s and 1970s. What were some of those achievements? Why did they leave so many women discontented? Why did some observers believe that the nation might be on the verge of a new women's rights movement?

Perspective 1

The Mixed Legacy of Women's Liberation

by Alvin P. Sanoff

Almost three decades after the birth of modern feminism, growing numbers of American women are suffering from a severe case of unfulfilled expectations. They have watched the bright promise of the '60s turn into the harsh reality of the '80s, leaving them not so much with new opportunities as with new responsibilities piled atop the old ones. Yet a look at women's history suggests that such periods of disillusionment often contain the seeds for the next stage of social change.

A new survey by the Gallup Organization documents the depth of the frustration. In 1975, the Gallup Poll found that only about one third of Americans thought men had it better than women. Today, that figure has jumped to 49 percent, with only 22 percent believing that women are doing better than men. Strikingly, 63 percent of those most affected by the feminist movement, women between the ages of 18 and 49, believe that men are better off. While a majority of those surveyed believe that the movement has made it easier for women to lead satisfying lives, 66 percent feel it is now harder for women to combine jobs and family, 76 percent that it is harder for marriages to be successful and 82 percent that it is harder for parents to raise children. "The women's movement made new opportunities available, but when women work 40 to 80 hours a week on the job in addition to working at home, then life is much more difficult," notes Betty Friedan, whose book *The Feminine Mystique* served as a catalyst for the women's movement.

Private solutions. Having dreams shattered is not a new experience for American women, as historians can testify. Throughout the 20th century, women's hopes have alternately been raised and dashed as periods of advancement have given way to decades of stagnation. Although the suffragette movement reached its goal in

149

1920, when women won the right to vote, that gain was promptly followed by an era of consolidation during which women struggled to work out family and career problems on their own. "Women turned to more privatized solutions," says University of Minnesota historian Sara Evans. "It was a time when lots of articles were written about having a career and a family at the same time."

After the upheavals of the Depression and World War II, women had to face the fact that gaining the vote did not automatically translate into equality in other spheres. "Women had assumed that achieving equal citizenship was the ultimate right," explains Ohio State University historian Susan Hartmann. "Then, 40 years later, large numbers of them recognized the extent of discrimination in the workplace." This recognition fueled the feminism of the '60s, which toppled barriers to equality in employment while raising the consciousness even of those who were not politically active.

Refueling for reform. The triumphs of women's "lib," however, soon gave way to the conservative Reagan era, during which most women again sought private solutions to personal dilemmas. Many turned to the mass media for advice and information. Some scholars blame the media, especially women's magazines, for making women believe that they could "have it all" without a price. That message is "nonsense," says Hunter College sociologist Ruth Sidel, but younger women now think that they can achieve like their fathers and simultaneously nurture like their mothers. If they fail, their disappointment may be even greater than that of the preceding generation because "their dreams are more extreme," argues Sidel, author of *On Her Own*, a new book about the conflicts faced by women.

Ironically, today's dashed expectations may foreshadow a revitalized women's movement. Hartmann, among other scholars,

Some women struggling to be wives, mothers, and pursue careers sometimes felt they were trying to do as much as had the individual commemorated by the statue in this cartoon.

believes that the nation will soon enter another cycle of reform, and it is in such climates that feminism has flourished. The rise of feminism in the '60s and '70s, for example, came on the heels of the civil-rights movement. In the next stage, Hartmann suggests, the movement will focus on such issues as care for dependents—both children and parents—and combatting violence against women. Others predict that the movement will try to bring about basic changes in the structure of work, so that both men and women can operate on more flexible schedules without raising the eyebrows of supervisors and colleagues.

[The] polling data from Gallup, while disheartening, indicate to Hartmann that women may be starting to realize the limitations of the gains they've made. "It is inevitable," she says, "that there will be a revival of the women's movement." No one knows how long it will take for the inevitable to arrive, but for millions of American women it cannot come soon enough.

The changes in the activities of women were clearly seen during the Persian Gulf war when women found themselves in combat situations.

AFTERWORD   Though no concerted movement with clear-cut goals had yet surfaced by the early 1990s, women at many levels continued to grapple with the problems of home and career. Issues of child care, equal salaries for equal work, and many others remained on the feminist agenda. In 1990, a new law made more federal money available for day care and also increased the tax credit for day care for low-income working parents with children. These changes helped, but for many working women day care remained expensive and hard to find.

From "The Mixed Legacy of Women's Liberation," by Alvin P. Sanoff. Copyright February 12, 1990, U.S. News & World Report.

THE STRUGGLE FOR WOMEN'S RIGHTS

INTRODUCTION   "The fitness and health craze" that Winifred D. Wandersee, professor of history at Hartwick College, described in the excerpt below from her book, *On the Move: American Women in the 1970s*, was still going strong as the nation entered the 1990s. The sense that women could succeed at any sport was no doubt heightened by the sight of gallant Joan Benoit winning the first Olympic marathon for women in 1984. And while the craze might have its unfortunate aspects, as Wandersee points out, it undoubtedly did produce a healthier group of Americans. What does she think were some of the good points of the pursuit of health and fitness? What were some of its less fortunate aspects?

Perspective 2

"You've Come a Long Way, Baby"

*by **Winifred D. Wandersee***

The fitness and health craze [that emerged in the 1970s] had an impact on both sexes, but what was unique was the extent to which women were engaging in physical activities that they had never before ventured to try. These included long-distance running, weight-lifting, and body-building, as well as aerobics, tennis, and a variety of team sports. The sight of an adult woman jogging through a public park or along a thoroughfare in shorts and T-shirt would have been greeted with ridicule and astonishment at earlier periods in American history. But by the mid-to-late seventies, it was a commonplace occurrence. Women were training for twenty-six-mile marathons as well as shorter road races. And most large cities had a "women's night" at their city park playing fields to provide for the growing number of women's softball teams.

Much of this was a positive reaction to women's liberation in the most literal sense of the term. Women were liberating themselves from the old conventional restraints on their physical capabilities and allowing themselves to participate in athletic endeavors on their own terms. But another part of the body consciousness of the seventies and eighties was less positive in its implications. Throughout the period women were obsessively concerned with body image, and this increasingly came to mean an obsession with slenderness—a physical characteristic that became practically a moral virtue in and of itself. Certainly the media—and especially television and women's magazines—encouraged this obsession. The ideal of "thin is beautiful" was promoted by using abnormally

152

thin models. The old adage "you can't be too rich or too thin" became the grounds for a new women's issue of the 1980s: the concern with eating disorders.

By the end of the 1970s a new image of womanhood had emerged—one that reflected some aspect of women's liberation but too often defined the successful woman in terms characteristic of an intensely consumer-oriented, individualistic, and competitive society that almost completely negated the true meaning and intent of feminism. The successful woman of the late seventies was envisioned as young and beautiful, slender, highly sexual but not necessarily monogamous, highly successful in some vaguely glamorous but undefined career, and just feminist enough to want her own way. She could be seen in the commercials on television and the advertisements in popular magazines—Virginia Slims, [Charlie] perfume, Jordache jeans, Diet Pepsi. She wore Maiden Form bras and sold perfume, sanitary products, shampoo, cars, fast food, and underwear. Her connection to the women's movement became increasingly hard to discern. Her relevance to the actual experience of most American women primarily reflected fantasy.

Women's public image was brighter, more visible, and more independent by the end of the decade. But ultimately, it was still controlled by the media which profited immensely from "women's

Charlie

A most original fragrance

Now the world belongs to Charlie.
The gorgeous, sexy-young fragrance. By Revlon

The Charlie perfume ads beginning in 1973 portrayed a new image of womanhood.

153

liberation" but managed to redefine it in individualistic, market-economy terms. The real meaning of the women's movement was lost to the public. And the image that had emerged became the target of moral conservatives and the New Right which attacked the movement on the grounds that it was immoral and selfish, destructive of family and the American way of life.

AFTERWORD   While some women may have carried the pursuit of thinness to extremes, the goal of health and fitness was certainly commendable. It was definitely better for health than the idea of the 1890s and early 1900s that a "full figure," such as that of comic-opera star Lillian Russell, was the proper goal of every woman (and man). And, although it may have had some negative effect, it was not clear that the media had manipulated the women's liberation movement as Wandersee suggests.

The pursuit of physical fitness started many women jogging.

From ON THE MOVE: AMERICAN WOMEN IN THE 1970s, W. Wandersee, pp. 172–74. Copyright 1988 and reprinted with the permission of Twayne Publishers, a division of G. K. Hall & Co., Boston.

A more favorable view of the media, in this case television, and the women's movement emerges in the recent *New York Times* piece written by staff member Joyce Purnick about the 1970s television program called "The Mary Tyler Moore Show" in which Moore played a working woman named Mary Richards. What were some of the lessons women—and men—could learn from this program?

Perspective 3

The Legacy of Mary Richards

*by **Joyce Purnick***

Mary Richards made it all O.K.—O.K. to be a single woman, O.K. to be over 30, O.K. to be independent. She even made it acceptable to stay home alone and watch her if you had a mind to, rather than go out on a date, the once-obligatory Saturday night date that women used to say they had even when they didn't.

Mary Richards was, of course, the charming television character that Mary Tyler Moore created in the 70's. Her show was intelligently written and acted, a pure treat every week. But, as its retrospective on CBS [in February 1991] reminded this dedicated viewer, it was much more.

Mary was a gentle role model, someone for the shaky career woman to identify with in the transitional 1970's. The show ran from 1970 to 1977 when, even though the women's movement was on its way, women were still expected to work between school and marriage and then put their jobs on hold after the wedding. If their lives didn't pan out that way, well, there was probably something a bit weird about them.

Mary wasn't weird. Not in the least. What was so endearing about her was that in a medium so well known for exaggerating, she was conventional and believable even as she knocked down stereotypes and barriers. She was Barbie Doll-pretty and slim, the way the ideal woman is supposed to be. But she had her frustrations and failures anyway and wasn't afraid to admit her impatience with the dating game. So did her friend Rhoda (Valerie Harper), who had an acknowledged weight problem. Before Oprah.

Subtly and sensitively, Mary's writers managed to address subjects as diverse as anti-Semitism and sexism without preaching, and without copping out. As tempting as it may have been to have Mary settle down into marriage, she didn't. She wasn't even divorced or widowed. Mary was television's first single working

155

The Mary Tyler Moore Show on TV made many women feel it was alright to be single and work. Here Mary is shown talking to her boss, Lou Grant, played by Ed Asner.

woman of significance who didn't have a standard explanation for her status.

She worked—because she worked. In fact, at a time when many young women were striving to establish themselves professionally, often at a price to their personal lives, Mary Richards' job was at the center of her life too—so much so that in the final episode, she said she no longer worried about treating her colleagues as family because, in a way, they were.

It's easy, 20 years later, to quibble about Mary's career. In the earlier years of the series she was little more than a glorified go-fer in a television newsroom. She worked for a man (Ed Asner's gruff-but-lovable Lou Grant, later the lead character in a show about newspapers), had trouble calling him by his first name and, though ultimately promoted to producer, didn't have a high powered job like her sit-com successor, Murphy Brown (Candice Bergen). But she was successful and capable, and even got Lou to give her a raise when she learned that a man had been paid more for the same job.

Doesn't sound like a lot now. But maybe, in a small way, that's because 20 years ago a fictional character on television made it O.K. for women to begin to come into their own.

AFTERWORD   While many feminists said that the women's movement still had numerous goals to achieve, the changes marked by "The Mary Tyler Moore Show" did indicate, as Joyce Purnick noted, that since the 1970s there had developed new attitudes about women, and wider opportunities for them.

From "The Legacy of Mary Richards," by Joyce Purnick, February 20, 1991. Copyright © 1991 by The New York Times Company. Reprinted by permission.

INTRODUCTION   In 1966, two sociologists at the Higher Education Research Institute at the University of California at Los Angeles began surveying student attitudes at a large number of colleges and universities. Their results were surprising, as writer and feminist Gina Allen reported in a "Feminist Update" in the *Humanist* magazine of January/February 1988. Why were college students so much affected by the women's movement? Why have women's successes had a substantial impact on men as well?

Perspective 4

Looking Ahead

*by **Gina Allen***

What do you think has most influenced college students in the years since 1966? The women's movement! This is despite the fact that, in the 1960s in particular, a great many causes were more highly visible and noisier than the quiet push for women's equality. There were the marches and sit-ins for rights for blacks and demonstrations for peace and an end to the killing in Vietnam. There was even an attempt to legalize marijuana….

Why have college students been so profoundly affected by the women's movement? For one thing, the first students studied [by sociologists in 1966] were part of the movement's beginnings, either because they wanted to be involved or because they couldn't avoid it.

In the late sixties and early seventies, women were making strides toward equality not only on campus but also in the workplace, as students found when they graduated into the real world. Even their homes of origin, their mothers, and their love lives were affected. Of all the revolutions that have ever occurred, the women's revolution is the most invasive of personal life. Changes for women mean changes for everybody. That's the big, unspoken reason why the Equal Rights Amendment has met with such resistance.

In the sixties and seventies, changes for women came rapidly. First came the Equal Pay Act of 1963, then Title VII of the Civil Rights Act of 1964, which banned discrimination against women and minorities in the workplace. Finally, the Higher Education Act of 1972 gave women equal rights to educational opportunities.

The impact upon colleges and universities was explosive. Quotas and "men only" policies at many universities, particularly

157

When wives worked outside the home, many men began to take on sometimes new and unfamiliar roles.

graduate schools, gave way. Women flocked to undergraduate accounting departments where once they were all but nonexistent. Today, a majority of accounting students are women moving on to become CPAs or MBAs. In the past fifteen years, the number of women in law schools has increased five-fold. In medical schools, the increase is 250 percent.

Changes for men have been slower but just as revolutionary, if not as well recognized. For students in college today, the changes have been taking place throughout their lives—which have paralleled the rise of the women's movement. They were the first Little Leaguers whose teams included both girls and boys. Many of them were brought up by feminist parents who encouraged them to be individuals rather than forcing them into gender roles.

In the sixties and seventies, it took anti-discrimination laws to give women choices. Choices for men are achieved through education and changes in custom. Young men in college today—and even in high school—are demanding the same choices that women have.

158

They want to be active parents as well as breadwinners or, in some cases, to leave the breadwinning to their wives while they stay at home with the kids and write the great American novel or practice the violin. They are asking colleges to help them prepare for parenting, and colleges are complying.

So, if you've been concerned that women are leaving the home for the workplace, take heart. Men are returning to the home as involved parents as they haven't since the Industrial Revolution. That's good for the kids and for the men, too. Taking time out from the competition of the marketplace to play with their children may just mean that men will live longer. And everybody in the family will live happier.

AFTERWORD   The transitions taking place for men and women in college were continued as the 1990s began. Some of the institutions that had been solely for one gender and had become coeducational were still trying to adjust to that major shift. The emergence of women's studies as a serious field at many colleges and universities was hailed by some and derided as unacademic by others. How all these changes would work out, how deep they were, and what their meaning would be to society as a whole were still questions to be answered as Americans moved toward the end of the twentieth century.

"Feminist Update: Looking Ahead" by Gina Allen, first appeared in January/February 1988 issue of *The Humanist* and is reprinted with permission of *The Humanist*.

THE STRUGGLE FOR WOMEN'S RIGHTS

INTRODUCTION   Phyllis Schlafly is a conservative activist who is strongly opposed to the feminist movement. She has a master's degree from Radcliffe College in Cambridge, Massachusetts, and a law degree from Washington University in St. Louis, Missouri. In the excerpt below from her book, *The Power of the Positive Woman*, she argues that marriage and motherhood are the best career for most women. What are her reasons?

Perspective 5

Marriage Can Make Women Secure

*by **Phyllis Schlafly***

arriage and motherhood are not for every woman, but before a young woman rejects it out of hand, she should give it fair consideration as one of her available options....

Are you looking for security—emotional, social, financial? Nothing in this world is sure except death and taxes, but marriage and motherhood are the most reliable security the world can offer....

Do you want the satisfaction of achievement in your career? No career in the world offers this reward at such an early age as motherhood. In the business or professional world, a man or a woman may labor for years, or even decades, to acquire the satisfaction of accomplishment. A mother reaps that reward within months of her labor when she proudly shows off her healthy and happy baby. She can have the satisfaction of doing her job well—and being recognized for it....

Marriage and motherhood, of course, have their trials and tribulations. But what lifestyle doesn't? If you look upon your home as a cage, you will find yourself just as imprisoned in an office or a factory. The flight from the home is a flight from yourself, from responsibility, from the nature of woman, in pursuit of false hopes and fading illusions.

If you complain about servitude to a husband, servitude to a boss will be more intolerable. Everyone in the world has a boss of some kind. It is easier for most women to achieve a harmonious working relationship with a husband than with a foreman, supervisor, or office manager....

If marriage is to be a successful institution, it must likewise have an ultimate decision maker, and that is the husband. Seen in this light, the laws that give the husband the right to establish the domicile of the marriage and to give his surname to his children are

160

good laws designed to keep the family together. They are not anachronisms from a bygone era from which wives should be liberated in the name of equality. If a woman does not want to live in her husband's home, she is not entitled to the legal rights of a wife. Those women who preach that a wife should have the right to establish her own separate domicile do not stay married very long. That "equal right" is simply incompatible with a happy lifetime marriage.

The women's liberationists look upon marriage as an institution of dirty dishes and dirty diapers. They spend a lot of energy writing marriage contracts that divide up what they consider the menial, degrading chores....

If you think diapers and dishes are a never-ending, repetitive routine, just remember that most of the jobs outside the home are just as repetitious, tiresome, and boring. Consider the assembly-line worker who pulls the same lever, pushes the same button, or inspects thousands of identical bits of metal or glass or paper, hour after weary hour; the stenographer who turns out page after page of typing; the telephone operator; the retail clerk who must repeatedly bite her lip because "the customer is always right."

Many people take such jobs because they need or want the money. But it is ludicrous to suggest that they are more self-fulfilling than the daily duties of a wife and mother in the home. The plain fact is that most women would rather cuddle a baby than a typewriter or factory machine. Not only does the baby provide a warm and loving relationship that satisfies the woman's maternal instinct and returns love for service, but it is a creative and growing job that builds for the future. After twenty years of diapers and dishes, a mother can see the results of her own handiwork in the good citizen she has produced and trained. After twenty years of faithful work in the business world, you are lucky if you have a good watch to show for your efforts....

Phyllis Schlafly was a vigorous and outspoken leader in the fight against the Equal Rights Amendment.

161

One of the mistaken pieces of advice often given young people is "be yourself." Maybe you are a hard-to-get-along-with person with an irritable disposition who spends the evening reciting and reliving the troubles of the day and blaming them on others. Don't "be yourself." Be the person you would like to be—a cheerful person who sheds a little sunshine into an otherwise gloomy day, who sees the silver lining in every cloud, who keeps a sense of humor in the face of every reverse. A cheerful disposition will keep a happy marriage decades longer than a pretty face. Men may like to watch a beautiful woman like Greta Garbo in the movies, but she is not the type of woman men marry or stay married to. Men choose and love the cheerful over the beautiful and the wealthy. Miss Garbo never married.

Pro- and anti-ERA demonstrators picketed in the Illinois State Capitol in 1978. Illinois never ratified the amendment.

AFTERWORD   Schlafly, who had, it seemed, found her own career defending marriage and motherhood, could not stop women from working. By 1990, 56 million, many of them wives and mothers, were on the job. Often, of course, they worked not from choice but because they needed the money.

INTRODUCTION   Betty Friedan's book *The Feminine Mystique* had helped to ignite the most recent women's movement. In the selection below from her 1981 volume, *The Second Stage*, she reviewed what the movement had so far accomplished and what the next stage should be. Why was the first stage necessary? Did she think it was completely over? What was the second stage to be?

Perspective 6

The Second Stage

*by **Betty Friedan***

The women's movement didn't start with heroics, or even with the political rhetoric of revolution. For me, as for most others, it started with facing the concrete, mundane personal truth of my own life and hearing the personal truth of other women—the "problem that had no name" because it didn't quite fit the image of the happy suburban housewife we were all living in those days—that image of woman completely fulfilled in her role as husband's wife, children's mother, server of physical needs of husband, children, home. That image, which I called the "feminine mystique," bombarded us from all sides in the fifteen or twenty years after World War II, denying the very existence in women of the need to be and move in society and be recognized as a person, an individual in her own right.

We broke through that image. So for nearly twenty years now, the words written about and by and for women have been about women's need to be, first of all, themselves...to find themselves, fulfill themselves, their own personhood...to free themselves from submission as servants of the family and take control of their own bodies, their own lives...to find their own identity as separate from men, marriage and child-rearing—and to demand equal opportunity with men, power of their own in corporate office, Senate chamber, spaceship, ballfield, battlefield, at whatever price. Organizing the women's movement, we broke through the barriers that kept women from moving, working, earning and speaking in their own voice in the mainstream of society. For nearly twenty years we have been pressing our grievances against men in office and home, school and field, in marriage, housework, even sex.

I remain committed to these unfinished battles. We had to do what we did, to come out of the shadow of the feminine mystique, and into our personhood, as women. We had to fight for our equal opportunity to participate in the larger work and decisions of society

In the photograph, a partial document reads:

Statement in support of the Equal Rights Amendment

ERAgram NOW

► PRESIDENT JIMMY CARTER
THE WHITE HOUSE
1600 PENNSYLVANIA AVENUE
WASHINGTON, D.C. 20500

MR. PRESIDENT, I URGE YOU TO MOBILIZE THE DEMOCRATIC
PARTY TO GET THE EQUAL RIGHTS AMENDMENT RATIFIED
BY THREE MORE STATES. THE LEGISLATURES OF ALL 14
UNRATIFIED STATES ARE CONTROLLED BY THE DEMO-
PARTY — YOUR PARTY. HUMAN RIGHTS BEGIN AT H

A VOTER WHO BE
YOUR CAM

ODAY!
m and mail to

While continuing to urge equality for women, Betty Friedan, shown here with another feminist leader, Gloria Steinem (on Friedan's right), began to feel that the women's movement needed other goals.

and the equality in the family that such participation entails and requires. This was the essence of the women's movement—the first stage....

There is no going back. The women's movement was necessary. But the liberation that began with the women's movement isn't finished. The equality we fought for isn't livable, isn't workable, isn't comfortable in the terms that structured our battle. The first stage, the women's movement, was fought within, and against, and defined by that old structure of unequal, polarized male and female sex roles. But to continue reacting against that structure is still to be defined and limited by its terms. What's needed now is to transcend those terms, transform the structure itself. Maybe the women's movement, as such, can't do that. The experts of psychology, sociology, economics, biology, even the new feminist experts, are still engaged in the old battles, of women versus men. The new

164

questions that need to be asked—and with them, the new struc-
tures for the new struggle—can only come from pooling our experience: the agonies and ecstasies of our own transition as women, our
daughters' new possibilities, and problems, and the confusion of
the men. We have to break out of feminist rhetoric, go beyond the
assumptions of the first stage of the women's movement and test
life again—with personal truth—to turn this new corner, just as we
had to break through the feminine mystique twenty years ago to
begin our modern movement toward equality.

Saying no to the feminine mystique and organizing to confront
sex discrimination was only the first stage. We have somehow to
transcend the polarities of the first stage, and even the rage of our
own "no," to get on to the second stage: the restructuring of our
institutions on a basis of real equality for women and men, so we
can live a new "yes" to life and love, and can *choose* to have children. The dynamics involved here are both economic and sexual.
The energies whereby we live and love, and work and eat, which
have been so subverted by power in the past, can truly be liberated
in the service of life for all of us—or diverted in fruitless impotent
reaction.

AFTERWORD   Many feminists disagreed vehemently with Betty
Friedan about what the next stage of the feminist movement should be.
Radical feminists wanted to continue the first stage and carry it through
to completion where women were truly equal to men and had all the
same freedoms. This stage would include not an acceptance of the family,
as Friedan urged, but a revision of the whole concept of the family so that
it could no longer, as they saw it, repress women.

THE NEW IMMIGRANTS

America—a promised land for people from all over the world—has been populated solely by immigrants. The earliest came from Asia thousands of years ago and are the forebears of the American Indians. Europeans and Africans only began to arrive millenniums later.

The First European Immigrants

Within the continental United States the first permanent European settlements were those of the Spanish, who founded St. Augustine in 1565 and Santa Fe in 1609, and the English, who established Jamestown in 1607. During the seventeenth and eighteenth centuries, many other Europeans came to what is now the United States—among them were English, French, Dutch, Portuguese, Spanish, Jews from many lands, Swedes, Welsh, Germans, Scots, Scotch-Irish, plus a small number of Finns, Swiss, Austrians, and Italians. The Africans were brought against their will. The thirteen colonies were a rich mixture of people from many lands even before the American Revolution.

Ten thousand people, largely Latin Americans, proudly became United States citizens in a mass ceremony in Miami, Florida, in 1984.

167

In the 1820s a wave of immigration began from Ireland, Germany and, later, Scandinavia. This came to be called the "old immigration." It continued until around 1882. In that same year immigration from China—long opposed by Californians—was stopped. Another act passed at that time forbade the admission of criminals, the insane, paupers, and others rated "undesirable" into the country. These were the first national laws to limit the flow of immigrants to the United States.

The First "New Immigration"

Restrictions were soon to increase. In 1921 the first immigration quotas based on national origin were enacted. Then in 1924 the National Origins Act aimed to reduce immigration to only 150,000 per year by 1929. The quotas in these laws were based on the ancestry of the people who were already in the United States. This favored immigrants from northern and western Europe over the "new immigration" from southern and eastern Europe. The 1924 act also excluded all Chinese, Japanese, and other Asians (except Filipinos, since their islands were then a possession of the United States). There was, however, no quota placed on Western Hemisphere countries (North and South America). These laws had set the nation on the path of tightly limiting the numbers of immigrants and where they came from.

Immigrants young and old come to the United States seeking a better life. This family arrived in Philadelphia around 1900.

The next significant change in immigration rules came in 1952 as Congress struggled with a new "Red [Communist] scare." The McCarran-Walter Act kept the old quota system, but using the excuse of "national security" it set up an insulting system of checks for "subversives"—even including people who wanted only to visit the United States. But more in keeping with American tradition, the act finally allowed Asians already in the United States to become citizens and it also permitted 2000 Asians to immigrate each year. In the 1950s and 1960s as well, people from many lands were given sanctuary in the United States, outside the quotas, as refugees from Communist persecution. Thousands of "Freedom Fighters," for example, were admitted from Hungary after their 1956 revolt was crushed by the Soviet Union.

PERSPECTIVES

The New "New Immigration"

In 1965 the immigration law was thoroughly revised. The Immigration and Nationality Act of that year was passed when the civil rights movement was in full swing. The new law abandoned the old quota system based on national origin that had favored northern and western Europe. Instead, it set a blanket annual limit of 170,000 immigrants from the whole Eastern Hemisphere, the only reservation being that no more than 20,000 could come from any one country. The nations of the Western Hemisphere for the first time were now given a quota, 120,000 a year, but unlike the Eastern Hemisphere, there was no cap on the number from any one nation. To guide decisions on whom to admit, the 1965 act made special provisions for uniting families. Lower on the preference scale were skilled workers and refugees.

Lawmakers believed that, even without quotas, the act would bring in immigrants who reflected the existing make-up of the United States. Two representatives of the American Legion explained the logic behind this opinion: "Nobody is quite so apt to be of the same national origins of our present citizens as are members of their immediate families." Since there were not many Asians in the United States, few arrivals of their relatives were predicted.

But the actual results came as a surprise. People from Asia, vigorously using the family-uniting clause, arrived in America in great numbers. One immigrant, over time, could bring in a dozen or more members of a large family. Here was the new "new immigration," the subject of this unit. The immigration from Asia—increased by refugees fleeing the Communists in Southeast Asia—added a new spice to the old American mix. Indian, Thai, and Vietnamese restaurants became a normal part of the American scene. These Asians, along with large numbers from Latin America, made up the new "new immigration."

The old problem of remarkable numbers of people entering the country illegally led to a revision of immigration law in 1986. Although its main target was Mexicans, there were thousands more who avoided border guards and slipped into the United States to live and work outside the law.

Mexicans, of course, had had a long and close association with the United States. Under the Treaty of Guadalupe Hidalgo in 1848, those who lived in the Southwest when it was seized by the United States in the war with Mexico were guaranteed their property rights and allowed to become U.S. citizens.

For many years, Mexicans moved back and forth across the border between the two nations at will, and even when the border became more controlled there was no quota for admission (although those who came without the proper documents were, of course, in the country illegally).

169

A group of immigrants from Russia was photographed on shipboard as they arrived in Boston in 1922.

While the 1965 law had introduced a limit of 120,000 on all Western Hemisphere immigration, many thousands of Mexicans were entering without legal permission and despite the border controls. Finally, the Immigration Reform and Control Act of 1986 attempted to deal with the problem of illegal aliens once and for all. In order to begin with a clean slate, this law allowed illegal immigrants who could prove they had been in the United States since January 1, 1982, to become legal residents. Then, to discourage others from sneaking across the border to find work, it imposed fines on employers who hired undocumented workers. In addition, our borders were to be more closely patrolled to keep out illegal aliens.

At first the 1986 law seemed to work well, as illegal immigration diminished. But then as time passed, people desperate for work once again found their way into the United States in large numbers. Now nearly a million were caught annually by the border patrol. How many were making it across safely, no one knew—one estimate put it at 200,000 each year. Clearly, the 1986 law was not enough.

In 1990, a new immigration act was passed that increased the number of immigrants allowed from Europe while not decreasing the flow from elsewhere. But this was certainly not the last time Congress would wrestle with the question of who, and how many, should be allowed to enter America and of what to do about the nation's porous borders.

INTRODUCTION   In July 1990 Richard Levine, a reporter for the *New York Times*, viewed the effect of the "new immigration" on the city of New York. He found many ways in which these newcomers were helping the city. What are some of these ways? Why have these immigrants not been a problem? Who might they have hurt?

———— ·✦· ————

Perspective 1

Young Immigrant Wave Lifts New York Economy

*by **Richard Levine***

For the fourth time in its history, New York City is being resettled and reshaped by migration.

The latest arrivals come largely from the Caribbean, Latin America, Asia and Africa. They have revived bleak sections of the Bronx and Brooklyn and built two new Chinatowns. They have taken fruit stands and stationery stores and fashioned them into commercial empires. They have filled low-skilled but crucial health-care jobs and may have preserved New York's garment industry.

But less evident than the proliferation of Chinese newspapers in street-corner kiosks or the Dominican flags flying from the aerials of livery cabs is the basic impact immigrants have had on the city's economy. The latest influx, which started in the 1960's, gained force during New York's remarkable economic comeback, providing a fresh source of youthful workers and helping to sustain the boom of the 1980's.

Economists say the city still needs young people to balance a native population becoming older and smaller. But in the period of economic stagnation that has descended upon New York, some wonder whether the immigrants will continue to arrive at their current rate, which approaches 100,000 a year, and, if they do, how well the city will be able to absorb them, at least until slack times end.

Inevitably, Some Hostility

Some worry as well about the prospects of immigrants already here, many of whom work in the machine shops and factories of the city's manufacturing concerns, a part of the economy that is shrinking rapidly. And the new immigrants have attracted hostility, as immigrants inevitably do, from sometimes less prosperous groups already living here.

171

Misunderstandings over the language and customs of newcomers sometimes create problems. This demonstration against a Korean market in Brooklyn in 1990 took place after a customer declared she had been mistreated by a clerk.

Eighteen countries sent 5,000 or more people to New York from 1980 to 1986, led by the Dominican Republic, Guyana, Jamaica, China and Haiti. The latest influx is far more varied than two previous waves of foreigners who came to the city, the Irish and Germans between 1840 and 1860, and the Italians, Poles, Russians and Greeks from 1890 to 1915, or for that matter the migration of southern blacks and Puerto Ricans after World War II.

With perhaps 2.6 million foreign-born residents in the city, about a third of the population, immigrants are already a huge consumer market that generates economic activity and jobs.

'We Trust Each Other'

The new immigrants have not had much of an impact on welfare rolls, experts say, and many take jobs as restaurant workers, hotel housekeepers and hospital attendants that are often spurned by native-born residents.

172

They have formed networks to help newly arrived compatriots to find employment and housing and to make their way.

"We trust each other, we understand each other," said Sali Nezaj, an Albanian who found work in the Bronx 20 years ago as a superintendent in an apartment building and now owns buildings, hiring others from his country to work in them.

Immigrants have rebuilt whole neighborhoods of the city, including Mr. Nezaj's Kingsbridge in the Bronx, Washington Heights in Manhattan and Elmhurst in Queens, some of them home to previous waves of foreign-born settlers.

"The empty stores become full, and the full stores become better," said Louis Winnick, a senior consultant at the Fund for the City of New York, who has written a book about Sunset Park in Brooklyn, a neighborhood settled and resettled by the Dutch and English, Scandinavians and Irish, Italians, Poles, Greeks, Puerto Ricans, Dominicans and, most recently, Chinese.

Without the latest wave of immigration, he said, New York would be "a boarded-up city."

Even so, Vernon M. Briggs, Jr., a professor at the New York State School of Industrial and Labor Relations at Cornell University, notes that some blacks who made up the third wave of migration are now returning to the South.

"I think immigration is part of what's pushing them back," he said.

Young Newcomers Lift 80's Economy

In the 1970's, as the latest wave of immigration was gathering, New York City suffered a deep and demoralizing decline, as factories fled to the South and middle class residents to the suburbs. The decade that followed brought a sharp turnaround as the city gained jobs and people.

Had it not been for immigrants, many economists say, the 70's would have been worse and the 80's, though largely driven by a boom on Wall Street, less impressive. From 1980 to 1987, for example, 575,000 immigrants to New York City replaced 375,000 native-born residents, for a net gain of 200,000 people.

"Certainly, in the 80's, it would have been tough to sustain the kind of expansion we had without immigration," said Emanuel Tobier, a professor at the Robert F. Wagner Graduate School of Public Service at New York University.

173

The new settlers vary educationally as well as ethnically and have filtered into a wide variety of occupations, from Indian physicians to Filipino nurses to Romanian knitters to Albanian building superintendents to Chinese garment workers to Haitian cabdrivers.

New immigrants opened stores, refurbished neighborhoods, and helped improve life in many cities. This Korean arranges the lush display of produce at his grocery store in New York City.

But they largely share one demographic characteristic: They are of working age. Some 60 percent are in the prime working years of 25 to 44.

The impact of so many relatively young people has been great. In the 1970's, immigration pushed up the potential labor supply slightly at a time the city's population was actually declining by about 1 million.

Among non-whites, employment rates also tend to be higher in foreign-born groups than in corresponding native-born groups. For example, 1980 census data indicates that 65 percent of black immigrants over 15 years old were employed, against 53 percent of native-born blacks in the same age group, and that 65 percent of Asian immigrants were employed, but 56 percent of native-born Asians.

174

"The people who come here are the most ambitious of the groups," Professor Tobier said. "They may sometimes look like poorly educated people to us, but they are more educated than those who don't leave. And they have a higher sense of self-esteem, of what they can do in the world."

"They have more of an incentive to work hard," he also said, "and less to fall back on, in the sense of the welfare system. They come here and feel they have to rely on themselves, and their own effort. They're not plugged into the social service system."

AFTERWORD   As New York entered a new financial crisis in the 1990s, it was not certain that the new immigrants would continue to come. But when prosperity should return, no doubt another wave of newcomers would seek the big city in hopes of improving their lives.

INTRODUCTION   Bill Barich, a writer of fiction and nonfiction, visited the border areas in both Mexico and California in 1990. There, he found, illegal immigrants who escaped the Border Patrol might be robbed and even killed by desperadoes on either side of the border. But still they came in large numbers. Why do they come? Why do you think they are willing to take any risks to make their way into the United States and, once there, do "anything at all"?

Perspective 2

La Frontera

*by **Bill Barich***

The most heavily travelled border in the world is a strip of scrubby California desert that runs for fifteen miles between the United States and Mexico, starting at the Pacific Ocean and ending at a thriving yet isolated spot called Otay Mesa. A chain-link fence follows the border for much of its course, but it is torn in many places and trampled in many others, and in some places it has fallen down....

Between the ocean and the mesa, the only town of any size is San Ysidro, California, just across from Tijuana. About forty-three million people pass through its legal port of entry every year, in vehicles, on bicycles, and on foot, but nobody knows for certain how many undocumented migrants slip illegally over *la frontera*. An educated guess would be about five thousand every day. They come primarily from Mexico and Central America, and they carry their most precious belongings with them in knapsacks or plastic supermarket bags. The Border Patrol, in its San Diego Sector—a territory roughly as big as Connecticut—apprehends about a third of them, logging almost fifteen hundred arrests every twenty-four hours, but the others drift on to Los Angeles or San Francisco or Sacramento, or to farms in the great Central Valley, staying with relatives and friends while they look for work. If they fail to be hired anywhere, they go farther north, to Oregon and Washington, ready to pick fruit or to gut salmon in a packinghouse, willing to do anything to earn their keep....

Joe Nunez [of the Border Patrol] is assigned to Brown Field Station.... [H]e is...an easygoing type, who likes a beer and a barbecue and doesn't let himself become hung up on the most salient metaphysical issue of this job—that is, whether or not the chaos at the border is intentional. Sometimes it troubles him that the job isn't more stimulating, and he thinks about transferring to an investigative unit in L.A., because the thrills at Brown Field are few

and far between. Nunez caught some Chinese illegals once, and once he caught some Yugoslavs, but then O.T.M.s (illegal aliens who are Other Than Mexican) are common in the San Diego Sector: in fiscal year 1988, its agents arrested (among others) three hundred and forty-seven Colombians, two hundred and sixty-six Brazilians, fifty-three South Koreans, twenty Indians, sixteen Turks, eleven Filipinos, seven Canadians, three Israelis, and one person apiece from Nigeria, Somalia, Gambia, Algeria, and France.

The chain-link fence along the border near San Diego does little to hinder illegal immigration into the United States.

One night, when the moon was almost full, Nunez let me ride with him on patrol. Only minutes after we left the station ...[Nunez caught five illegals].

"Where are you from?" Nunez asked.

The oldest-looking man answered..."Oaxaca," he said. Oaxaca is home to Mixtec and Zapotec Indians. It is sixteen hundred miles to the south, and its hills are so eroded that a corn crop, which has always been a staple of the Indians, can scarcely be grown there anymore.

"Why are you crossing?"

The man shrugged. "To work," he said.

Trabajar—to work. All night, whenever Nunez asked "Why are you crossing?" the word was repeated. People wanted to work, and they didn't care what the work was like. They would do stoop

THE NEW IMMIGRANTS

Mexican migrants do many hard jobs United States citizens do not want. These workers were picking peppers in Florida.

labor, wrecking their backs and their knees picking strawberries or artichokes, and they would prune vineyards and orchards that had been sprayed with pesticides. They would swab floors, bathe infants, scrub pots and pans, and breathe in formaldehyde vapors in factories where particleboard was made. They would sell bags of oranges from traffic islands in Santa Monica, and they would hammer dents from bumpers at auto-body shops in Glendale. Contractors would employ them to dig ditches for foundations. They would agree to remove asbestos from around heating ducts and to scrape lead-based paint from walls. They would pour hot tar for roofs, handle beakers in methamphetamine labs, mow lawns, deliver circulars, clean sewers—anything at all.

AFTERWORD   Clearly, the people who illegally cross the border are hard workers who suffer in their pursuit of a better life. It is probable that the border could be closed, but that would damage our neighbor, Mexico, whose people need work, and deprive Americans of some inexpensive labor. So the United States continues a policy of halfway enforcement of the law. Perhaps this is why Officer Nunez did not want to say whether or not all "the chaos at the border is intentional."

From "La Frontera." Copyright © 1990 by Bill Barich. First appeared in *The New Yorker.*

INTRODUCTION   Mortimer B. Zuckerman is the editor-in-chief of *U.S. News & World Report* magazine. The selection below was written while Congress was debating immigration reform in 1990. Zuckerman calls for an increase in the number of immigrants with special skills. Under the 1965 law, spouses, parents, and minor children are given special preference outside the quota system, but under the quota system the law also gives preference to other family members. Zuckerman opposes this. Why does he think the admission of more young, skilled workers would be good for America?

Perspective 3

Give Us Your Brainpower

*by **Mortimer B. Zuckerman***

Ellis Island, the historic gate through which 17 million foreigners walked to become Americans between 1892 and 1943, recently reopened as a museum after a spectacular restoration. It is a fitting moment since Congress is now reviewing immigration policy for only the third time in our history. It should draw inspiration from Ellis Island. The 100 million descendants of those 17 million now account for 40 percent of our population. They defined America by lending muscle and brain to the transformation of a nation from a 19th-century agrarian society to the dominant industrial power of the 20th. One generation of German refugees developed electricity, another nuclear energy. As historian Oscar Handlin wrote: "Once I thought to write a history of the immigrants in America. Then I discovered that the immigrants were American history."

Do people still want to come? You bet. In 1987, the U.S. opened a special "visa lottery" for citizens of countries that had been short-changed by immigration quotas. Ten thousand were allotted; 1.4 million people applied. America can pick and choose the best—but we no longer do. Paradoxically, just at the time when knowledge is increasingly the key to prosperity and power, we have placed more limits on that category of immigration than any other. Only 10 percent of the available visas are reserved for people with the skills we need. The criterion that counts today is family reunification. It accounts for more than 90 percent of new admissions. In 1989, only 15,000, to 20,000 people—roughly 3 percent of all immigrants—were selected because of their high skills. Yet, even such a small number still provided almost half of all immigrating mathematicians and computer scientists, more than one third of the engineers

179

Thousands upon thousands of immigrants entered the United States through Ellis Island in New York Harbor. The registry building is shown here after its recent restoration. It is now a museum.

and university professors, and 3 of the 10 nurses. They saved us $1.5 billion in education costs.

Policy must be refocused to benefit our nation economically. A much higher number, as many as half of the available visas, should be set aside for applicants who can fill shortages in fields such as engineering, medicine, computers and other sciences.

Both the Senate and House bills allow for increases in total immigration from the current 540,000. The House bill is preferable because it sets a higher cap—775,000 vs. 630,000 in the Senate version. But it is too heavily weighted in favor of family integration, increasing from 436,000 to 520,000 the number of family-based immigrants annually. Unrestricted immigration of the immediate relatives of U.S. citizens—that is, spouses, aged parents, and minor children—should continue for humanitarian reasons. But nepotism should not be the standard for so many of the increased numbers of visas. Everyone knows that the "family" category is abused.

The Senate bill increases to 150,000 the number of visas based on skills. These should be increased to at least 250,000 and then stepped up, gradually, to represent half of our immigration. The new law should also earmark at least 10,000 visas for those with proven financial skills and capital. Such a program has been in place in Canada for 10 years. In 1988, such foreign entrepreneurs

180

invested nearly $2 billion in new enterprises in Canada, creating an estimated 15,000 jobs.

Opponents of the open door portray immigrants as either welfare recipients or job stealers. All the recent studies prove the opposite is true. Immigrants tend to be energetic, talented self-starters. They draw very lightly on Social Security and medicare, and virtually the same as natives do on other kinds of welfare spending. The result is a smaller drain on the public purse, compared with Americans, during their first dozen years in the U.S.

Studies by the Urban Institute and the Rand Corporation also establish that immigrants do not deprive Americans of work. In fact, they create jobs, sometimes helping ailing businesses stay alive. The only areas where they held wage increases down slightly were those that were filled almost exclusively by immigrants. Furthermore, the admission of young, payroll-tax-paying immigrants reduces the dependency of the elderly on too few workers in our Social Security system. Not one of the economists who recently reported on immigration concluded that greater immigration would have a negative effect; 80 percent felt it would be positive.

Engraved on the base of the Statue of Liberty is Emma Lazarus's poem "The New Colossus." It reads in part: "Give me your tired, your poor, your huddled masses yearning to breathe free." To which we might add: "Give me your educated, your energetic, your scientifically and technologically proficient, your bearers of investment capital, yearning to work hard."

AFTERWORD   Despite Zuckerman's plea, many labor leaders bitterly oppose the immigration of skilled workers, fearing that it will cost American workers their jobs, and possibly weaken unions as well. Other critics feel that since many Americans are unemployed, especially in our central cities, instead of admitting immigrants these people should be trained and put to work.

From "Give Us Your Brainpower," editorial by Mortimer B. Zuckerman. Copyright October 29, 1990, U.S. News & World Report.

THE NEW IMMIGRANTS

INTRODUCTION   Richard D. Lamm, in his third term as governor of Colorado in the mid-1980s, with Gary Imhoff, a writer on immigration and minority issues, wrote *The Immigration Time Bomb: The Fragmenting of America*. The authors were alarmed that the increasing Latino immigration was altering American society. In what ways did Lamm and Imhoff think the current immigration was different from those that had gone before? Were they opposed to all immigration? What did they think the government should do?

Perspective 4

The Splintered Society

*by **Richard D. Lamm** and **Gary Imhoff***

I love America, and I want to save and preserve it. To most people, that sentence would seem a bland and non-controversial bit of flag-waving. But when the subject is immigration, a lot of people would object to it strenuously. When confronted with the social stresses and strains that large-scale immigration place on our country, some people just want to ignore them, want to deny that they exist. Others are less well disposed to the culture and the mores of the United States and don't believe that we should save and preserve them.

Let me say it directly: massive immigration involves serious and profound social and cultural dangers. The United States is not immune to the trends that have affected and altered all other human societies. Civilizations rise and civilizations fall—and there are certain universal pathologies that characterize the fall of history's civilizations. Ethnic, racial, and religious differences can become such a pathology; they can grow, fester, and eventually splinter a society. The "melting pot" society is clearly an exception to history's lesson, and we make a serious mistake if we think that all our differences can and will harmonize (or homogenize) without our work and care.

I believe that America's culture and national identity are threatened by massive levels of legal and illegal immigration. Admittedly, there are good historical reasons that some people remain complacent in the face of massive migration. After all, there were adjustment difficulties in earlier periods of peak migration, but the fears of Americans that migrants would permanently change the basis of American culture were unjustified, as were their fears that migrants and their children would not assimilate. And the yearly inflow of immigrants to the United States composes

182

a lower percentage of our total population today than it did in the 1910s. Therefore, it is easy to assume that we're unjustified if we worry about the social effects of large-scale migration today.

I know that earlier large waves of immigrants didn't "overturn" America, but there are at least five reasons not to be complacent, reasons to believe that today's migration is different from earlier flows. First, the yearly inflow of immigrants is a small portion of our society's total population, but immigrants are not evenly dispersed throughout the country. They settle in a few big cities, and they constitute large proportions of those cities. The culture of Kansas and Nebraska is not much affected by the small influxes of migrants they receive, but the cultures of Miami, Florida; Los Angeles, California; and Washington, D.C., have been and are increasingly affected, visibly and markedly.

Second, the peak migration years of the 1910s were ended in 1921 by a new immigration law that set annual ceilings on migration levels. The peak immigration years of the 1970s and 1980s are continuing—and there is not now any plan that promises to end them. The migration stream of the 1910s would not have been assimilated had it continued unabated, had it been augmented by decades of followers.

Third, earlier flows of immigrants were well mixed by language groups, and no single group predominated. As Michael Teitelbaum pointed out in an influential article: "While there were substantial concentrations of a particular language group in past decades (e.g., 28 percent German-speaking in 1881–90 and 23 percent Italian-speaking in 1901–10), previous immigration flows generally were characterized by a broad diversity of linguistic groups ranging from Chinese to Polish to Spanish to Swedish. Furthermore, those

So many Cubans settled in Miami, Florida, that one area was called Little Havana, after their island's capital.

THE NEW IMMIGRANTS

concentrations that did occur proved to be short-lived." But, Teitelbaum points out, today's migration stream is quite different: "The INS reports that, in the period 1968–77, approximately 35 percent of all legal immigrants to the United States were Spanish-speaking. If one adds to this figure plausible estimates of Spanish-speaking illegal immigrants, it becomes clear that over the past decade perhaps 50 percent or more of legal and illegal immigrants to the United States have been from a single foreign-language group." And this concentration shows no sign of changing in and of itself at any time in the near future.

Fourth, today's migrants come after the impact of the ethnic pride movements in America, after the death (or at least during the long critical illness) of the melting pot ideal. During the last peak of immigration to the United States, our society insisted on immigrants' assimilation. If adult migrants who settled with others of their own nationality were not required to learn English by the circumstances of their lives, at least their children who entered public schools were certainly expected—by their parents as well as by society—to make English their primary language. Today, with ever-growing language group subcultures, assimilation is controversial, and pressures within immigrant communities countervail against the attractions of assimilation.

This photograph shows San Francisco's famous Chinatown. With the new immigration, Chinatowns in many American cities are growing and even multiplying. New York City now has three.

Fifth, the argument that we need not worry about the assimilation of massive migrant groups ignores our actual experiences with immigration over the past decade. In fact, there have been numerous and profound problems in cities where recent large movements have settled. There has been a recent and threatening history of cultural clash and conflict, a record of widening community rifts, a new splintering of our society that results directly from large and continuing immigration—legal and illegal....

184

Certainly, the culture of the United States will change in the future. It has changed in the past. Our culture and social organization have evolved in many ways. Every immigrant group has changed America just as every group has been changed in the process. Current waves of immigrants will change this country. What is important is the pace of change. We in the United States wish to regulate the pace of that change, to ensure that it will be an evolution rather than a revolution based on population changes. We wish to enjoy the healthy invigoration we experience from absorbing new residents from many cultures; we don't want to suffer the radical overturning of our way of life or the clash and conflict of differing cultures within our country. And only a reasonable, moderate pace of immigration into the receiving cities, already saturated themselves with problems and splintered culturally and economically, will ensure that we can meet that ideal.

AFTERWORD   Lamm and Imhoff were concerned that the flow of immigration was not evenly distributed. Some cities, like San Diego, California, San Antonio, Texas, and Miami, Florida, had a single "minority" who were, in fact, the majority. And many other communities were noticeably altered by the presence of large numbers of people from one country or region. Lamm and Imhoff were particularly disturbed by what they saw in Miami, Florida, where it was said that a citizen could live without ever needing to know any language except Spanish. They felt this changed America in an unacceptable way. They were not, as they made clear, opposed to all immigration, but they did not want the new arrivals to create a divided society, whose members were unable even to speak the same language.

From THE IMMIGRATION TIME BOMB by Richard D. Lamm and Gary Imhoff. Copyright © 1985 by Richard D. Lamm and Gary Imhoff. Used by permission of the publisher, Dutton, an imprint of New American Library, a division of Penguin Books USA Inc.

INTRODUCTION   Some results of the Immigration and Nationality Act of 1965 were reported by *Newsweek* magazine in September 1990. It also revealed many hidden issues in our immigration policy. Why do some experts believe we need immigrants? Why are other people opposed? What are the hard questions legislators have to face?

Perspective 5

America's Changing Face

by **Tim Mathews** *with* **Anne Underwood** *and* **Clara Bingham**

The transatlantic age of immigration has given way to something new. More immigrants now come to the United States than ever before. About 10 million poured out of the '80s, more even than the 8.8 million who arrived between 1900 and 1910.[1] Of these, 89 percent were Europeans in 1910; today that number has dwindled to 10 percent. After 1965, when the immigration laws lifted national quotas and gave more emphasis to reuniting families and taking in refugees, Hispanic and Asian immigrants became the largest contingent of new Americans. The Immigration Reform and Control Act (IRCA) of 1986 swelled the ranks further by accepting more than 3 million people illegally working the fringes of the American economy.

Professionals in the fields of labor and immigration believe that increasing legal immigration (but throttling illegal immigration) contributes to a healthier economy and a higher standard of living. Gene McNary, commissioner of the Immigration and Naturalization Service, says, "There is a pretty good argument that we need these people to complement our aging work force." He believes a healthy economy can absorb up to 1 million immigrants each year.

Politicians find it much easier to act against illegal immigrants than to sort out the conflicting equities and advantages of legal immigration. But even in this field the results have been modest at best. For a time after IRCA took hold, increased border patrols appeared to be cutting illegal immigration from Mexico by 30 to 40 percent; but current numbers now seem to be heading back to where they were in the early 1980s. Jeffrey Passel of the Urban Institute in

---

[1] Proportionately, however, immigration in the first decade of the century was much greater, amounting to one in every ten people. To equal that number in the 1980s, 25 million immigrants would have had to come to America. *Eds.*

Washington calculates that 2 million to 3 million illegal immigrants still live in the United States; he believes their numbers grow by about 200,000 a year.

IRCA may also be contributing to racial discrimination. The government's General Accounting Office has reported that some employers are using the threat of INS fines to avoid hiring anyone who even looks like an illegal immigrant. One GAO survey found that 19 percent of the employers surveyed were involved in "a serious pattern of discrimination" against nonwhites. "Congress has made a huge mistake in assuming that employee sanctions would solve the problem of illegal immigration," says Cecilia Muñoz, a lobbyist for the National Council of La Raza, the Hispanic rights group. The law does help some newly legalized workers. But it has pushed others into new sweatshops.

The way to reform immigration policy is to start with a dry-eyed view of economic reality. Our productivity has fallen. The country doesn't have enough skilled workers.... A report prepared for the Department of Labor by the Hudson Institute predicts that the American labor force will expand by only 1 percent annually in the 1990s. By the year 2000, the average American worker will be 39 years old. As the country shifts to a service economy, it will need more skilled workers. Part of the solution could be to increase the number of skilled immigrants.

This approach has some negative side effects. Susan Weber, of Zero Population Growth, says America's population is already too big to live off its own natural resources and is despoiling the environment and burying itself in waste. "We need to send a message to other countries that you need to take care of your own numbers," says Rose Hanes of Population-Environment Balance. "You cannot use the United States as a safety valve."

The views of some others are not so reasonable. "We should start reducing quotas before we become a Third World country," says David Duke, once of the Ku Klux Klan, now a Republican state

The long borders of the United States are crossed illegally by many people every day. These men were caught in Arizona in 1986 and returned to Mexico. They would probably try again.

187

legislator in Louisiana. Duke blames everything from crime to declining standards of education on immigrants; he says when he delivers his message on TV, thousands of Americans call to support him.

Free-market theorists disagree. Julian L. Simon, the author of "The Economic Consequences of Immigration," a recent book, argues that immigrants "make us richer, not poorer, stronger, not weaker." Simon points out that immigrants tend to have a stronger work ethic than many native-born Americans. He rejects the biases of people like Duke. "It is in our genes that we are against foreigners," he says. "Some use fancy words like 'nativism,' but at the root of most opposition to immigration is plain racism."

It is vitally important to improve the American labor pool. The problem is to decide how. The economy and labor market are so fluid that it is difficult to predict which skilled workers are sure to be needed. With our aging population, nurses will be in short supply; but it is hard to plot any other occupation so cleanly. Prognosticators foresaw a shortage of engineers at the very moment they were failing to anticipate the end of the cold war. Now companies are laying off engineers.

This refugee dentist from Vietnam now practices his profession in California, assisted by his wife and sister.

One of the hardest choices is whether to use skilled immigrants as a quick fix or to start rejuvenation closer to home. "When you have inner cities crammed with people who need work, our obligation should be to educate and train people in America first," says Rep. John Bryant, a Texas Democrat. Demetrios Papademetriou, director of Immigration Policy for the Labor Department, thinks it would be wise to encourage employers to correct their past mistakes. He would offer them incentives to retrain their existing work force, improve wages and tap new sources of labor like the disabled. Doris Meissner, a former INS official, also believes we need improved training and education. "It is harder to change when there is an oversupply of immigrants," she says. "You need tension to improve the system." One practical approach would include a measured increase in immigration, while keeping regulations flexible and subject to constant review, instead of freezing them into laws that last a quarter century.

The Senate has passed a bill calling for a new system that would award points toward admission to immigrants who are young, who have advanced educations, who come from 36 countries, mostly in Europe, and who have skills needed in key industries. The proposal has run into opposition from ethnic groups who charge that it reintroduces a double standard in favor of whites, particularly Irish immigrants. Putting greater emphasis on the quality of immigrants would allow the United States to compete more favorably with Canada and Australia for highly educated and skilled newcomers.

The House, sensitive as ever to ethnic and business lobbies, is working on legislation that offers something for everyone. Its buzzwords are "diversification" and "equalization." The idea is to admit more skilled immigrants without cutting back the flow of relatives joining their families. This would require raising the present level of immigration from 530,000 to 775,000 annually. The Senate would admit 630,000. The outcome will depend in part on whether a recession begins over the next few months. But in all likelihood, the future will see the arrival of more skilled immigrants and more Europeans. As one Senate staffer puts it, "Few members of Congress are out there speaking for immigration control. If you do, you are considered anti-American dream."

AFTERWORD   Congress was unable to decide anything in the new immigration law of 1990, except to increase the number of migrants from Europe. In total 700,000 would be admitted annually from around the world in 1992–1994, after which the number would drop to 675,000. Still, the debate over how many people should be admitted and whether preference should be given to family unification or skilled laborers continued. Some critics insist that the flow of immigrants must be reduced to enable the United States to absorb all its new members. Others urge that immigrants will not only do many jobs that native-born Americans refuse to do, but that those with special skills are vital to our labor pool.

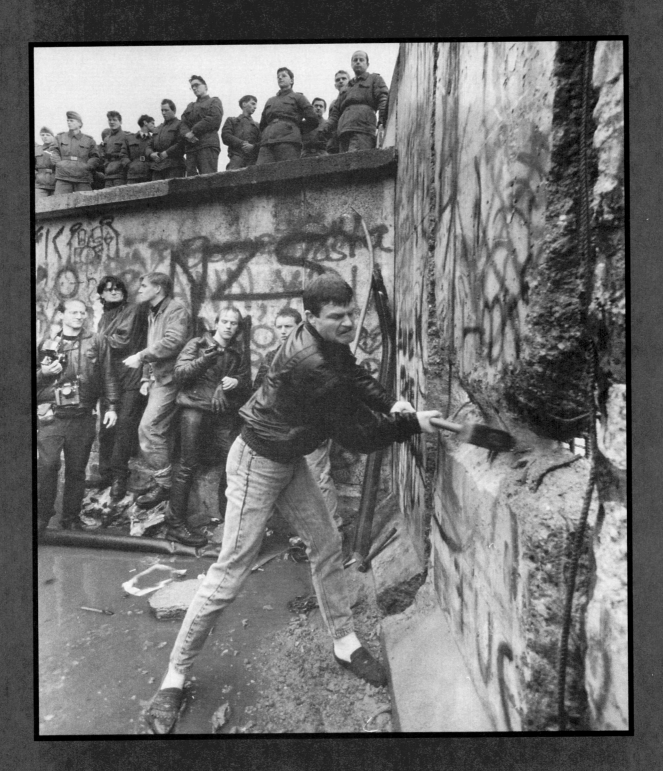

Perspectives on

AFTER THE COLD WAR— WHAT NEXT?

FROM THE EDITORS

In 1945 as the victorious armies of the Soviet Union, Great Britain, France, and the United States crushed Germany between them, the shape of the Europe to come was on every leader's mind. Joseph Stalin, the ever-suspicious Soviet dictator, was determined to see that the Soviet Union's western flank was protected by a string of friendly states. He also wanted to make certain that Germany would never again be a threat, as it had been twice in just twenty-five years.

At the same time, Great Britain's Prime Minister Winston Churchill was urging the United States to keep its troops in a part of Germany which had earlier been delineated as the Soviet zone of occupation. He hoped to use these forces as a bargaining chip. "Nothing really important has been settled," he wrote the new American President, Harry Truman, "and you and I will have to bear great responsibility for the future." Despite Churchill's warning, the United States withdrew its forces to its own zone.

Soon after East Germany opened its borders to West Germany, happy Berliners began to attack the hated wall dividing their city.

191

The Beginning of the Cold War

When Harry Truman came to the Presidency upon the death of Franklin D. Roosevelt, the warnings of Churchill and of some of his advisers quickly convinced him that the USSR was extremely dangerous and that he must "get tough with Russia." Upon meeting Soviet Foreign Minister V. M. Molotov less than two weeks after taking office, Truman lectured him about the Soviet Union's failure to carry out the Yalta agreements to allow the Polish people to choose their own government. Molotov began to deny the President's appraisal of the situation, only to be interrupted by Truman. The President insisted that if the Soviet Union wanted friendly relations with the United States it must carry out its commitments. Molotov protested, "I have never been talked to like that in my life."

"Carry out your agreements," Truman bluntly replied, "and you won't get talked to like that."

The interchange between Truman and Molotov was a weather vane indicating the future. Though the wartime alliance did not immediately collapse (the United States still wanted the Soviet Union to enter the Pacific war), distrust was evident on both sides.

Some historians have felt that had the United States been more understanding of the Soviet Union's anxiety, the cold war might have been averted. That is, however, a minority view. A less skeptical attitude on the part of the United States perhaps could have made the "cold" conflict less heated. But it seems unlikely that the Western powers could have persuaded the Soviets to give up their Eastern European satellites, their belief in the inevitable triumph of communism over capitalism, or their historic fear of the West.

The opposition of East and West, the division of Europe (and especially of Germany), the arms race, the balance of terror caused by thousands of missiles armed with nuclear warheads—all these were essential elements in the cold war that had dominated the world's history ever since World War II. These conditions lasted long enough so that they began to seem the natural order of things. Western leaders made ritual sounds of complaint, but they did not expect much to change. In fact, while they no doubt wanted better relations with the Soviets, a slowdown in the arms race, and a reduction in nuclear weapons, the leaders were reasonably comfortable with the way things were. Indeed, they were quite upset when Reagan and Gorbachev at their meeting in Reykjavík, Iceland, in 1986 seemed to come close to doing away with *all* long-range nuclear weapons. The cold war had brought 45 years of peace to Europe—nearly twice as long as the peace between the first and second World Wars. If the cold war ceased, what might take its place?

The End of the Cold War?

In 1989 the old arrangements collapsed with astonishing speed. Unnoticed by most of the West, the Soviet Union had been steadily weakening, at first under the tired leadership of Leonid Brezhnev and then from a lack of direction, as the tenures of Yuri Andropov and then Konstantin Chernenko were cut short by death. When Mikhail Gorbachev came to power in 1985 he was alarmed to find the already weak Soviet economy being drained further by the war in Afghanistan, the arms race, and the need to keep millions of men in uniform to control its satellites and to counter the West.

Gorbachev, it seems, quickly concluded that the Soviet Union could only be saved by ending the cold war. As early as 1986, he reversed the Brezhnev doctrine which had proclaimed that the Soviet Union and their Eastern European Communist satellites had a right to invade one of their number if it followed policies that might hurt other members of the bloc. The Soviets used this doctrine to justify sending troops into Czechoslovakia in 1968.

Ronald Reagan and Soviet leader Mikhail Gorbachev were all smiles when they met to begin their talks in Reykjavík, Iceland, in 1986.

Gorbachev announced instead that the Soviet Union had "unconditional respect" for the right of every country "to choose the paths and forms of its development." And when the test later came, it was clear that he meant it.

No doubt everything changed far more swiftly and completely than Gorbachev expected. But when the Communist governments of Eastern Europe collapsed in 1989, the Soviet Union did not interfere. This was probably due to the severity of the USSR's own problems.

What would happen now? Would Gorbachev himself fall? Would the Soviet Union collapse? In 1990, Latvia, Lithuania, and Estonia declared their independence and others seemed ready to follow. The Soviets refused to let them leave. Mighty forces that had long been suppressed, such as nationalism and ancient ethnic hatreds were now on the loose throughout the old Soviet bloc. Where all this turmoil would end was hidden in the future. In the selections that follow you will find a variety of views of what that future might hold.

AFTER THE COLD WAR—WHAT NEXT?

INTRODUCTION   Ronald Steel is professor of international relations at the University of Southern California. In the selection below, published in July 1990, he describes some of the changes occurring in the wake of the transformations in Europe. Why does he think we might "wax sentimental about the cold war"? What does he see as the significant changes brought about by the end of the cold war?

Perspective 1

The Rise of the European Super-power

*by **Ronald Steel***

L et us, for a moment, wax sentimental about the cold war. Expensive and often irrational as it was, it did at least provide a few benefits. Among these were a Europe that was politically stable for the first time in this century, a German state that neither dominated nor threatened its neighbors, and an extraordinary degree of American influence over the richest and most populous nations of the continent. The superpowers made the big decisions about war, peace, and diplomacy; they negotiated with each other not as members of a team, but as franchise owners. Our alliance, NATO, was of course voluntary and democratic, while that of the Soviets, the Warsaw Pact, was enforced by the Red army. But despite these great differences it was still accurate to speak of "our" Europe and "their" Europe.

That is gone. The passing of the cold war means not only a truce, or even entente, between the "superpowers" (the very phrase now sounds dated and self-promoting), but the demise of a political order run from Washington and Moscow. Today we, like the Soviets, find ourselves increasingly confined to the sidelines as Europe organizes and defines itself. From the cocoon of the cold war a new Europe is metamorphosing into a form we cannot easily predict or control....

As these conditions have eroded, so has Atlanticism [America's policy built on European dependence and the Atlantic alliance]. With the Soviet Union transformed from an "evil empire" into an impoverished and confused supplicant, American protection has become less important to Europeans. Needing us less, they are no longer so accommodating to our wishes. Our place in Europe's consciousness is shrinking. As we assume our new role as kibitzers at the political and economic reorganization of Europe, we find ourselves immersed, however regretfully, in a post-Atlantic world.

Although the passing of the old order relieves the fear—always exaggerated—of a Soviet invasion of Western Europe, it also unleashes problems repressed by the struggle of the giants. The cold war may be over, but...the competition of nations and the quest for power are not.

Thousands of workers marched in Paris on January 12, 1991, to protest the threat of an allied attack, led by the United States, on Iraq.

AFTERWORD   The decline of the Soviet Union and the rise of a powerful new Europe, as Steel pointed out, created a different world, but they did not end "the competition of nations and the quest for power." As Europe went through the pangs of a new birth, the United States had to learn how to live in a world where the relationship of states and even the nature of nations were changing. Would Czechoslovakia split into Czech and Slovak nations? Would Yugoslavia fall apart? Could the Soviet Union survive?

From "The Rise of the European Superpower," by Ronald Steel, July 2, 1990. Reprinted by permission of THE NEW REPUBLIC, © 1990, The New Republic, Inc.

AFTER THE COLD WAR—WHAT NEXT?

INTRODUCTION   In the selection below, Robert G. Kaiser, assistant managing editor for National News for the *Washington Post*, views the great changes taking place in Eastern Europe and the Soviet Union. What are some of the weaknesses he says the West failed to see in the East? What are some of the problems the Soviet Union and the nations of Eastern Europe must now overcome?

Perspective 2

Eastern Europe and the Soviet Union

by Robert G. Kaiser

Energies suppressed for decades by the arbitrary power of communist parties have suddenly erupted in every nation of the old Soviet Empire, causing a political earthquake. Earthquakes in nature occur when pent-up energy in two plates of the earth's surface becomes so powerful that the plates must move. In the old Soviet bloc, the energies are political, economic, sociological, even psychological. If there were a Richter scale for disruptions in modern societies, the temblor [earthquake] we are witnessing might well set a record for the entire history of nations.

The forces being released are so great that their consequences are genuinely unpredictable. Uncertainty about what comes next is the subtext of nearly every public pronouncement by the new leaders of Eastern Europe, including Mikhail Gorbachev. Uncertainty should also be the theme of any outsider's attempt to analyze these changes. What began in 1989 will be a feast for students of politics and economics, probably a font of great literature, too, and certainly a splendid intellectual entertainment. But it will take years to see these changes whole; now we have only clues about where they may lead.

The world, East and West, got so used to the old arrangements that most of us lost sight of just how unnatural they were. Arbitrary, authoritarian regimes, dependent for their power on secret police forces, and large communist parties, insisting on counterproductive economic policies and demanding adherence to an irrational orthodoxy, created bizarre societies. All of these societies have missed out on most of the dramatic technological changes that have transformed the capitalist world in the last generation. We called the Soviet Union a superpower without regard for its total failure to adapt to the computer age, for example. We agonized about the military threat from the East without seriously calculating the disarray in Soviet-bloc armed forces whose troops were appallingly trained, demoralized, badly equipped. As the shrouds and blinders have fallen away,

196

all in the West can finally see these countries more or less as they were: poor, corrupt, stupidly run, spiritually bankrupt, mired in a bureaucratic morass, committed to economic programs that destroyed the environment of each of the seven nations of the Soviet bloc while failing to make any of them remotely competitive by international standards.

The collapse of ancien régimes throughout Eastern Europe and the crumbling of the old order in Moscow are rightly a source of jubilation, but none of the changes now occurring can wash out the stains of 45 years, or 75, of Marxism-Leninism. Throughout the old Soviet Empire, workers have learned how to prove the accuracy and relevance of the old Russian joke: We pretend to work, and they pretend to pay us. Economies that have so long devalued both work and money cannot be quickly turned around. All crave the silver bullet of Western investment, and all are likely to get it. Then all will also learn that investment cannot undo the consequences of so many years of mismanagement and bad work habits.

Can Soviet peasants who have never managed a piece of land from season to season—or taken responsibility for decisions about

The primitive state of the economies of Eastern Europe was clearly revealed after the fall of the Communist governments there. These farmers with their long scythes were photographed in Romania.

197

what to plant, how to fertilize, and the like—learn to be efficient farmers? Can workers protected from economic discipline by ideology adapt to conditions where hard work is required and laziness is severely punished? Can workers unfamiliar with insecurity cope with unemployment? Can managers at every level of society, from the factory canteen to national ministries, learn to manage on their own initiative, without reference to higher authority or an ironclad rule book? Can a new class of politicians learn the value of tolerance and the ability to endure criticism or attack from rivals without resorting to repression? Can journalists learn to report information that the authorities would prefer to suppress, and will the authorities tolerate its publication? These are huge questions; the fate of the nations of Eastern Europe will depend on how they are answered.

The Soviet Union, Poland, Hungary, Czechoslovakia, Romania, and Bulgaria will now become a giant laboratory of politics, economics, sociology, and psychology. (East Germany seems destined simply to be absorbed into the Federal Republic.) A series of fascinating experiments will be conducted in this new lab.

While the opening of the first McDonald's in Moscow in January 1990 drew huge crowds, American companies found doing business with the bureaucrats of the Soviet Union and Eastern Europe extremely difficult.

AFTERWORD   Kaiser makes clear some of the daunting problems faced by the Soviet Union and the Eastern European nations. Yet there are the additional threats from ethnic rivalries and hatreds, from national claims and ill-defined borders, as well as the impatience of people who want a better life right away. When the Soviet empire collapsed, a Pandora's box was opened revealing countless problems, old and new. Even economically powerful West Germany, which swallowed East Germany on October 3, 1990, found far more difficulties than it had expected.

From Robert G. Kaiser, "Eastern Europe and the Soviet Union," *SEA-CHANGES: American Foreign Policy in a World Transformed,* Nicholas X. Rizopoulos, Editor, (1990: Council on Foreign Relations Press, NY), pp. 22–24.

198

INTRODUCTION As the United States prepared for possible war with Iraq in late December 1990, the editors of the *New Republic* magazine looked at the Soviet Union and speculated on its future. What did they identify as some of the problems facing Gorbachev? Why do you think they concluded that the United States and Europe needed to be concerned over events in the Soviet Union?

Perspective 3

Separation Anxiety

by the editors of the **New Republic**

With the United States on the brink of war in the Persian Gulf, Americans haven't been able to spare much attention for a crisis that is less immediately acute but in the long run certainly as momentous, possibly more so: the continuing, and increasingly chaotic, dissolution of the Soviet Union. The process makes front-page news often enough—as it did when Mikhail Gorbachev called for citizen vigilantes to stop black marketeers and installed a former KGB man and the ex-commander of Soviet forces in Afghanistan to run the Interior Ministry—but there's little discussion about what America's response should be. If there's famine, this country will want to help alleviate it. But what's the best way to do that? And as the Soviet Union, which has already ceased to be Soviet (in the sense of being Communist), ceases also to be a Union, and as real power drains away from Mr. Gorbachev's central government, shouldn't the U.S. government be placing more of its bets on the various republics? In any case, the United States is under no moral obligation to help prop up the crumbling edifice of the prisonhouse of nations.

All the signs are that the multiple economic and political crises of the Soviet Union are rising toward some kind of crescendo in 1991. Food prices at unofficial markets have tripled during the last year in Moscow. So have the hours people spend waiting in line to buy what little is available at state stores. People are working less and tempers are frayed—not only because of the shortages, but because the citizenry knows that the system, not nature, is to blame. Food exists. When it's not spoiling in storage or in transit, it's being hoarded in the countryside or diverted from the state distribution system for sale on the black market. The obvious solution is the non-black market: give farmland to the peasants, let middlemen buy from them and sell in town, turn illegal "profiteers" into

199

AFTER THE COLD WAR—WHAT NEXT?

legal entrepreneurs and make them compete with each other, thereby putting some eventual restraint on prices. But Mr. Gorbachev keeps postponing the plunge.

Fourteen of the fifteen Soviet republics have passed sovereignty declarations, in effect refusing to take orders from Moscow. (The exception is Kirgizia, which is nevertheless negotiating recognition pacts with Russia and other republics.) There are constant disputes about whose law takes precedence, which does nothing to dampen public cynicism. The possibility of serious violence is growing. Latvia is refusing to allow electricity to flow into installations of the Soviet army. Anti-Russian agitation in Kirgizia, on the Chinese border, has caused 40,000 to flee this year. The president of Azerbaijan appealed on Soviet TV to the secretary general of the United Nations and to President Bush, asking for peacekeeping forces (including U.S. Marines!) to protect his province from Armenia. The city council of Lujansk, in the Ukraine, has announced that it will secede and join Russia if the Ukraine becomes an independent country. The Ukranian government says such secession will be put down by force.

During the winter of 1991, in the face of uncertainty over the government's economic plans, goods disappeared from store shelves in Moscow and other Soviet cities.

Meanwhile, the political chaos is interfering with production, causing real shortages of medicine, electricity, and trucks. The rate of violent crime has exploded in the cities—up 49 percent this year in Belgorod, 55 percent in Kharkov—and the rate of unsolved crime has doubled, according to a recent Interior Ministry report. Politicians quarrel over ideology and policy, and sometimes just over power.... And Mr. Gorbachev, like a mechanic trying to get a hopeless lemon to start, opens the hood of the Soviet Constitution every six weeks or so and tinkers, expanding the nominal powers of

200

his unelected presidency even as his rivals and the population pay steadily less heed to his decisions....

Europe and America have an obvious practical interest in doing what they can to ensure that the manifold changes convulsing the territories of one-sixth of the globe be carried out as peacefully as possible. But it does not necessarily follow that they have a corresponding interest in the maintenance of the Soviet Union as such. Indeed, there is some great justice at work in the erosion of the world's last great empire. The odds for a supranational state of any kind are not good. And a supranational state held together by coercion would inevitably be unstable or repressive or both. Payments from the West would do little to make it any less of a threat to its neighbors and its own citizens alike. If a supranational state—or, more likely, a loose federation—is to be, it will have to be founded on voluntary association. And that means the republics must be free to go. And should they choose association with European nations rather than with their former comrades-in-chains, they must be free to do that, too.

AFTERWORD   In March 1991 Gorbachev won approval of a vaguely worded referendum in favor of preserving the Soviet Union. But six of the fifteen republics boycotted the voting and others added resolutions that undercut it. A land of over 120 different nationalities and many different languages, the Soviet Union has never been easy to hold together. Later in the article, the *New Republic* editors suggested that the United States should establish consulates in all the republics in order to be prepared if the union disintegrated.

From the editorial, "Separation Anxiety," December 24, 1990. Reprinted by permission of THE NEW REPUBLIC, © 1990, The New Republic, Inc.

INTRODUCTION   Lawrence T. Caldwell, the author of the selection below, is professor of political science at Occidental College in California. He describes the results of a 1990 meeting between the leaders of the Soviet Union and West Germany to try to agree on the unification of East and West Germany and on the relationship of a new German state to NATO. The Western nations wanted Germany to be part of NATO, while the Soviet Union favored its neutrality. What were the results of the meeting? What did it mean for the United States?

Perspective 4

Soviet-American Relations: The Cold War Ends

*by **Lawrence T. Caldwell***

On July 16, 1990, Soviet President Mikhail Gorbachev and West German Chancellor Helmut Kohl emerged dressed in cardigan sweaters and smiling broadly from their meeting at a resort in the Caucasus mountains. Their relaxed demeanor replicated the informal diplomatic style assiduously cultivated by recent American Presidents, a style designed to communicate confidence, friendliness, even an image of alliance rather than adversarial relations.

Their smiles were well deserved. They had just concluded agreements ending months of intricate bargaining and maneuvering first over whether the Soviet Union would sanction a reunited Germany, and then whether a unified Germany would become a member of the North Atlantic Treaty Organization (NATO). President Gorbachev had made an important concession: the new Germany could join NATO and Soviet troops would be withdrawn from their East German bases within "three to four years." Even more dramatic was the statement by Chancellor Kohl at that same news conference that after reunification "all the rights and responsibilities of the Four Powers will end." There in the Soviet Caucasus mountains, a West German Chancellor and a Soviet President had brought to an end the bitter struggle over a peace treaty ending World War II—a settlement that had divided the victorious allies of that war for 45 years, had shaped the societies of victors and vanquished alike and had several times brought the world to the brink of another world war.

The absence of the President of the United States gave the Soviet–German summit special meaning. Indeed, the next day in Washington, D.C., President George Bush carefully sanctioned the outcome of the Kohl–Gorbachev agreement and claimed some of the credit. Nonetheless, the meeting in Zheleznovodsk symbolized a

202

changing world. For Gorbachev it represented the culmination of five years of hard work to ease the confrontation in Europe between NATO and the Warsaw Pact (the alliance of Soviet bloc states), and it affirmed his recognition that the forces of history that he himself had kindled in East Europe were moving at a pace and in a direction that he could no longer resist.

The agreement also symbolized new realities for Washington. Throughout the preceding year, President Bush's administration had reacted to developments initiated elsewhere. American power seemed very much on the sideline, or at least in the background. The revolutionary changes of 1989–1990 began in Moscow, Prague, Budapest, Bucharest, Warsaw and Berlin. Although the President of the United States seemed reduced in stature by these history-making events, George Bush and Secretary of State James Baker radiated a kind of calm and competence that reassured their own citizens and those of allied states as well.

While Washington seemed almost peripheral to the drama of the past year, Moscow was at its center. President Gorbachev had spun a web of change, and although he could not control every event that landed in it, no one doubted that he was the pivotal figure. His agenda seemed richer with critical decisions and the pace of his activity seemed greater than any figure in modern history.

West German Chancellor Helmut Kohl (seated right) and Soviet President Gorbachev (seated center) were in jovial moods during a pause in their talks in July 1990 over German membership in NATO.

AFTERWORD   On September 4, 1990, World War II officially ended. The occupying powers—Great Britain, France, the United States, and the Soviet Union—gave up their occupation rights and left East and West Germany free to combine. A new united Germany was born on October 3. It immediately became the largest and strongest power in the European Community. In October 1990, it was announced from Sweden that President Gorbachev was awarded the Nobel Peace Prize.

From "Soviet-American Relations: The Cold War Ends," by Lawrence T. Caldwell. Reprinted with permission from *Current History*. © 1990 Current History, Inc.

AFTER THE COLD WAR—WHAT NEXT?

INTRODUCTION   Writer John Newhouse in the *New Yorker* magazine of August 27, 1990 described a Europe where "events, not governments, have taken charge." Why did no one think Germany would be unified so quickly? Why does Newhouse believe these momentous changes are "hard on the Soviet Union"? Why are they also difficult for the United States?

Perspective 5

Sweeping Change

*by **John Newhouse***

A week is a long time in politics, and a few weeks can be an eternity, as the world discovered last autumn when the postwar order was abruptly pushed aside, to be replaced by who knows what. As in 1945, Europe stands on the threshold of an era—a time when the restless energies of states will be released in ways that defy easy comprehension, let alone prediction. Although much of the talk of devising a new European architecture is resolutely sensible, it is for now only that—talk. Events, not governments, have taken charge. They are being shaped by the interplay of a Soviet Union spinning out of control and a unified Germany that, besides being big and rich, will revert to behaving like a fully sovereign nation-state, as distinct from a more or less compliant, guilt-ridden loser of the last great war. German self-esteem is on the rise, and one of the few certainties out there is that a united Germany will be authentically German—certainly more so than the Federal Republic has been.

The good news—warm peace supplanting cold war—is being obscured by the general confusion of most governments. With no compass, the various helmsmen are relying on flash judgments and, in some cases, the biases of yesteryear. Moreover, the ripple effect of Saddam Hussein's coup de main in the Persian Gulf, besides transforming the Middle East and much of world politics, has made the start of the post-Cold War era even murkier. The year 1989 belonged to Eastern Europe, and many diplomats in Europe and elsewhere reckoned that the focus in 1990—and perhaps the decade of the nineteen-nineties—would be on a prosperous European Community (E.C.) as it adapted to a more preëminent German role and a reduced American presence. But other diplomats and foreign-policy specialists have felt that the nineteen-nineties would be dominated by conflicts between Third World countries—more and more of them lethally armed—that would be struggling over resources, not ideology.

204

A year ago, the prospect of a unified Germany hadn't turned up on any government's horizon, including Bonn's. To the contrary. Officials everywhere had convinced themselves that the issue lay far ahead—well into the next millennium. Most Germans, after all, wouldn't put at risk the prosperity that had been gained westward in the European Community, or the security provided by the North Atlantic Treaty Organization, for the risks and uncertainties of union with East Germany. Even if East Germany should be willing to become an appendage of the Federal Republic, they believed, it would be unable to switch from a command economy to a market economy. West Germany's allies had supported unification rhetorically, but the continued division of Germany was tacitly embedded in the policies of each of them. And, in any case, Moscow could be counted on to veto unification. So it seemed.

All this is hard on the Soviet Union. First, it gave up control of Eastern Europe—the buffer zone between it and Western Europe, which it had sought since the time of Catherine the Great. Now it has lost what was gained in 1945 from "the great patriotic war"—the division of Germany into zones, one of them Soviet-run. Although the Soviet Union has won some Olympic gold medals and has got into space, it is acutely aware that its system has had only two true successes: building nuclear weapons and defeating the Germans. What's more, in having to accept what its old enemy is about to do, it has to swallow forty years of its own propaganda: Germans are Fascists and revanchists [seekers of revenge for their military defeat], NATO is a certain aggressor, and so on. The political pain (and perhaps the cost to leadership) of having to acquiesce in a unified Germany joining NATO is hard to overstate. Moscow is exacting a price for this from Western governments, but it is the Germans themselves who are paying a large part of the price—in Deutsche marks. The political cost to the West generally isn't yet clear.

In September 1990 representatives of the allies that defeated Nazi Germany in 1945 met with representatives of East and West Germany to give up their occupation rights. Pictured here (left to right) are four of the foreign ministers, Eduard Shevardnadze of the Soviet Union, James Baker of the United States, Hans-Dietrich Genscher of West Germany, and Douglas Hurd of Britain.

205

With the end of the cold war, the United States no longer needed to keep as many troops in Germany. This air station was one of the bases slated to close.

The new situation in Middle Europe is also hard on America, custodian and beneficiary of the postwar order. Protecting its allies has been the country's vocation for four decades. Overnight, that role lost much of its relevance, and the change means, among other things, that a great many of the American troops deployed in Europe will be coming home.... From now on, Washington will have to exercise its influence bilaterally and through institutions like the E.C., of which America is not a member, and larger groups, like the thirty-five-member Conference on Security and Coöperation in Europe, or C.S.C.E., in which America's vote has had no special weight. As for American interests in Europe, they are no less vital, even if they, too, are somewhat changed. With Germany a budding colossus, and the E.C. on the verge of becoming a unified market of three hundred and twenty-five million people—the industrial world's largest—and even now pursuing monetary union and a common currency, America's political and economic stake in this evolving Europe is all the greater. And a continuing American military involvement in Europe is logical, since, whatever befalls the Soviet Union politically, the strength of its armed forces will vastly exceed that of Western Europe's.

AFTERWORD The transformations in Europe were far more difficult for the Soviet Union to adjust to than they were for the United States. Many military officers and old-line Communist bureaucrats were unhappy, while the Soviet people grew ever more distressed by the failure of *perestroika* to put food and goods on store shelves. In several republics ethnic groups were killing each other. The changes President Gorbachev had started now threatened to destroy him.

From "The Diplomatic Round: Sweeping Change," by John Newhouse, August 27, 1990. Reprinted by permission; © 1990 John Newhouse. Originally in *The New Yorker*.

INTRODUCTION Brian Crozier, a columnist for the conservative magazine *National Review* had thought once before that the cold war was ending. This made him cautious in November 1990 about predicting that it was now all over. As he viewed a weakened Soviet Union that appeared to need American aid to survive, what indications led him to believe that the cold war had not completely ended? How did he think the United States ought to behave?

Perspective 6

All Over? Not Quite

*by **Brian Crozier***

Before me as I write is the issue of *NR* [*National Review*] dated March 16, 1973. It shows COLD WAR in graphic blocks of ice, melting. The title: "The End of the Cold War?" The author? No prizes....

Seventeen years after my cover story, the general consensus has removed the question mark, and not for the first time. In the eyes of earlier sages,... the cold war was already over in the 1960s, courtesy of Nikita Khrushchev.

Today, journalists and politicians alike refer daily to "the post-cold-war period," meaning now. So, is "The Protracted Conflict" truly over at last, third time round? My answer is: No, not quite. What has happened is that the Soviet Union, which in 1944 launched what [James] Burnham called World War III, precursor of the cold war, has been spectacularly losing it over the past few years. I wish I could say that we, the West, have been winning, but that's not the way it is.

The clues to Mikhail Gorbachev's strategy are all there, if we will only take the trouble to look. First: Gorbachev is a Leninist. He has said so, repeatedly. In a virtually unreported speech on February 13, 1987, he compared the disastrous situation at that time with the situation Lenin faced in 1918, which forced him to sign the Treaty of Brest–Litovsk with the victorious Germans. Like Lenin, comrades (he said, in effect), we will make sacrifices, and resume our forward march later.

His talk of a "common European home" is strictly Leninist, as is his current parasitical coexistence: hoping the West will pay for the free market which, kicking and screaming, he is now being forced to inject into the sclerotic Marxian economy.

There is, however, a big snag: only tiny, feeble attempts have been made so far to convert the enormous Soviet arms industry to civilian needs. In a speech at the 28th Party Congress on July 3 [1990], Foreign Minister Eduard Shevardnadze made two shattering revelations.

The first was that the Soviet Union had been spending 25 per cent of its GNP on "defense" (far higher than the highest CIA estimates). His other revelation, however, was more directly relevant to the Protracted Conflict/Cold War/Peaceful Coexistence issue. Indeed, he provided us with yet another synonym for our thesaurus. Over the past twenty years, he said, the Soviet Union had spent 700 *billion* rubles on "ideological confrontation" with the West. Divide by twenty, and you get a cold-war budget of 35 billion rubles a year. True, Moscow cab drivers don't take rubles these days, but even if you do some deflationary arithmetic, you get a tidy sum going to active measures, disinformation, and dirty tricks. In other words, to the cold war.

Now, up to the present, there is absolutely no sign that the vast machine handling this kind of activity has been dismantled. Indeed, it is

Boris Yeltsin was the rising star of Soviet politics as the decade of the nineties began. He was a problem and an irritant to Mikhail Gorbachev, president of the Soviet Union.

known to be ticking over, mainly but not entirely in Third World countries. And it would be surprising if it were not so, considering that the restructuring of this apparatus was Gorbachev's top priority under *perestroika*.

So, do we really want to pay for the cold war to continue? If we do, then we shall provide financial aid to the Soviet Union without linkage. If we don't, the relevant linkage is easy to define: it means the verifiable disbanding of Service A (for Active Measures) of the KGB and the rest of the cold-war apparatus.

PERSPECTIVES

If you say that this is impossible so long as the unelected Party and its unelected president are still in office, then I can only agree. The system is unreformable. Be kind to History: let the system die. Let something new take its place: perhaps a commonwealth of Slavic States (Russia, the Ukraine, Byelorussia), with peripheral republics (Georgia, Azerbaidzhan, Armenia, Uzbekistan, etc.) linked with it or not. In this set-up, Boris Yeltsin, the man who tore up his Party card, will be the new man the West can "do business with" (to quote Mrs. Thatcher's unfortunate phrase).

AFTERWORD   Boris Yeltsin had once been a highly placed Communist official and a close follower of Mikhail Gorbachev. He was demoted by Gorbachev for pushing too aggressively for more rapid and radical reform toward democracy and a market economy. But the political changes instituted by President Gorbachev allowed Yeltsin to be elected chairman of the Russian republic's Parliament in 1990. He then became louder in his criticisms and even called for Gorbachev's resignation. His popularity with the people, who had lost confidence in Gorbachev, was a mounting challenge to the Soviet president. In 1991 Yeltsin became the first popularly elected president of the Russian Republic.

From "All Over? Not Quite," by Brian Crozier, November 5, 1990. © 1990 by *National Review*, Inc., 150 East 35th Street, New York, NY 10016. Reprinted by permission.

Glossary

Abolitionist *n.* a person seeking the legal end of slavery in the United States

acerbic *adj.* harsh or biting in tone

acquiesce *v.* to give in quietly

adherence *n.* steady, firm attachment or support

adversary *adj.* involving opposing parties or interests

affirmative *adj.* positive

affirmative action *n.* steps taken to increase the representation of women and minorities, especially in jobs and higher education, often by the use of timetables or quotas

agrarian *adj.* relating to the land or the farmer and farm life

alien *n.* a citizen of a foreign country

allusion *n.* an indirect reference; a hint

ambiguous *adj.* not clear; uncertain; vague

amity *n.* friendship

anachronism *n.* someone or something that is not in its proper historical time

ancien régime *n.* [French] a governing system that no longer exists

anti-Semitism *n.* prejudice against Jews

apologia *n.* a defense, justification, or apology for actions or opinions

appeasement *n.* conciliation; pacification

appropriations *n.* money formally set aside for a specific use

arbitrary *adj.* not limited or restrained by any law or standard

assiduous *adj.* unceasing, constant

assimilate *v.* to join the cultural tradition of a group or population; to make similar

astigmatic *adj.* having faulty or distorted vision

atrophy *v.* to waste away, decline

authoritarian *adj.* relating to a system in which power is concentrated in one person or a small group

Beneficent *adj.* doing kind, generous acts

bilateral *adj.* having two sides or parties

black market *n.* trade in goods in violation of official regulations

Black Power *n.* the call in the late 1960s for blacks to exert their political and economic power to achieve social equality

bloc *n.* a group of nations, businesses, or people working together

blues *n.* slow songs originated by American blacks that have distinct harmonic and rhythmic patterns

boycott *n.* the refusal to deal with someone or something in an attempt to force a certain result

broadsheet *n.* a large sheet of paper printed on one side as an advertisement

bureaucracy *n.* the unelected officials who run all the departments of a government

Capital *n.* money or property used, or available for use, in a business

capitalism *n.* an economic system in which the means of production and distribution of goods are owned by individuals

carnage *n.* bloody and extensive slaughter, especially in battle

c'est la guerre [French] "that's war"

circulation *n.* the average number of copies of a publication sold over a given period of time

coalition *n.* temporary alliance of separate groups for joint action

coexistence *n.* living together without hostility or conflict, despite differences

cold war *n.* a rivalry between nations that stops short of open warfare

colossus *n.* anything extremely large or powerful

commensurate *n.* corresponding in extent or degree

commodity *n.* something that can be bought, sold, or traded

communism *n.* a system of social organization where the state holds all property in the name of the people

compassion *n.* a feeling of sorrow for the problems of others accompanied by the desire to help

compatriot *n.* a fellow countryman or countrywoman

consignment *n.* a system in which a business pays the producer for goods only after they are sold

consulate *n.* offices of the consul who is appointed by a country to look after its interests and its citizens in a foreign country

consumerism *n.* an emphasis on the buying of consumer goods

consummated *v.* brought about to completion; finished

contemplate *v.* to think about intently

contempt *n.* the feeling of scorn toward something or someone considered low or vile

cornet *n.* a valved instrument somewhat similar to a trumpet

cornucopia *n.* a great amount; abundance

coterie *n.* a small group of people with a common interest

countervail *v.* to exert equal force against

coup de main *n.* [French] a surprise attack

criterion *n.* a standard on which a decision or judgment can be based

De facto *adj.* existing in fact, not by law (de jure)

deficit spending *n.* spending public funds raised by borrowing rather than by taxation

delineate *v.* to sketch out or define

demagogue *n.* a leader who uses popular prejudices and false promises in order to gain power

demographic *adj.* relating to statistical data on human populations

denominational *adj.* under the control of a particular religious body

deride *v.* to ridicule

despotism *n.* a government system in which the ruler has unlimited power

détente *n.* a French word meaning relaxing or easing; in diplomacy, used especially to refer to an easing of tensions between nations

diabolization *n.* represented as being wicked, evil, devilish

diplomacy *n.* the conduct of relations between nations

discrete *adj.* separate; distinct; individual

discrimination *n.* prejudice for or against someone based on race, religion, sex, or other classification

disillusionment *n.* state of being disenchanted, without illusion

dispassionate *adj.* free from emotion or bias

dispersion *n.* a spreading in all directions

disseminate *v.* to spread throughout

diversify *v.* to spread into or involve several different areas

domicile *n.* a place of residence; home

durables *n.* long-lived goods, such as refrigerators

dynamics *n.* all the varied forces which produce motion or change in any field

GLOSSARY

Ecumenical *adj.* general, universal

edifice *n.* a building, usually large

egalitarian *adj.* favoring equal rights

egregious *adj.* markedly bad in some way

elitism *n.* belief in the leadership of a superior group

entente *n.* an understanding or agreement between nations

entice *v.* to tempt

eon *n.* an immeasurably long period of time

ephemeral *adj.* lasting for a very short time

epitomize *v.* to typify

equalization *n.* an even distribution

equilibrium *n.* a state of balance

erroneous *adj.* mistaken; wrong

escalation *n.* increasing step by step

escapism *n.* mentally avoiding reality

evolution *n.* a theory which contends that all species developed from earlier forms and that natural selection determines which forms will survive

expansionist *adj.* pursuing additional territory

expediency *n.* seeking one's own advantage, often without regard to right or wrong

expenditure *n.* outlay, disbursement, spending

expositor *n.* one who explains

Facade *n.* a front, sometimes false

famine *n.* an extreme shortage of food

feminism *n.* a theory of human relations based on the belief in the political, economic, and social equality of the sexes

filial *adj.* of or befitting a son or daughter

fission *n.* the splitting of the nucleus of an atom, resulting in the release of large amounts of energy

fortissimo *n.* in music, a loud passage or note

free enterprise *n.* the system under which private business operates for profit without government interference beyond regulation necessary to protect the public

frontera *n.* [Spanish] frontier

fundamentalist *n.* one who believes in the Bible as literal truth

Gamut *n.* the entire range or extent

ghetto *n.* in America, a part of a city where members of a minority group live as a result of social or economic pressure

gramophone *n.* a phonograph

guerrillas *n.* irregular armed forces

Harmonic *adj.* in music, relating to the arrangement and regulation of tones sounded together

Icon *n.* a symbol

ideology *n.* the body of beliefs or ideas of a person, group, etc.

idiom *n.* the specific way in which a certain people or writers put words together to express meaning

immemorial *adj.* beyond the reach of memory or record

immigrant *n.* a person who enters one country from another country with the intention of settling

immigration *n.* the movement of people from other countries into a country

imperial *adj.* describing an empire or an emporer

imperialism *n.* the attempt to create or maintain an empire either by force or through economic or political dominance

improvise *v.* to compose and perform at the same time, without preparation

impunity *n.* protection from punishment

incendiary *adj.* causing, or capable of causing, fire

incisive *adj.* sharp; keen

indictment *n.* the act of charging someone with an offense

indigence *n.* extreme want or poverty

indiscriminate *adj.* careless in choosing

inertia *n.* resistance to action or change

inexorable *adj.* unable to be moved or influenced by persuasion; unrelenting

innovation *n.* a new idea, device, or method

insurgent *adj.* involved in a revolt

integration *n.* bringing individuals of different groups into society as equals

intervention *n.* interference; intrusion

intransigent *adj.* uncompromising

inure *v.* to accustom to accepting something undesirable

Jazz *n.* type of American music, developed primarily by Southern blacks from ragtime and blues, characterized by strong rhythms, ensemble playing, and improvisation

Kibitzer *n.* a giver of unwanted advice

kiosk *n.* small, light structure with one or more open sides, such as a telephone booth or newsstand

Laissez faire *n.* the doctrine that government should interfere as little as possible in economic affairs

lame duck *n.* an elected official whose term is about to end, and whose successor has been chosen but has not yet taken office; thus, someone who is no longer effective

left wing *adj.* showing liberal tendencies in politics

liberalism *n.* a political philosophy based on belief in reform or progress in politics, religion, etc.

liberation *n.* the act of setting free; freedom; equality

Machiavellian *adj.* of or relating to Niccolò Machiavelli (1469–1527) who advocated expediency in statecraft

manifold *adj.* many; varied; diverse

mass consumption *n.* widespread use of consumer goods or services

materialism *n.* the belief that physical things are most important in life

metaphysical *adj.* highly abstract; theoretical

microcosm *n.* a smaller group or system that stands as an example of a larger world

millennium *n.* an ideal time; one thousand years

monogamous *adj.* having only one mate

morass *n.* a marsh; swamp

mores *n.* the accepted customs and practices of a society

Napalm *n.* a highly inflammable jellylike substance

nationalism *n.* a special loyalty and love of one nation above all others

nativism *n.* a policy of favoring native inhabitants over immigrants

negativism *n.* an attitude characterized by the questioning of accepted beliefs

nepotism *n.* favoritism shown to one's relatives in hiring

normalization *n.* restoring to a natural or normal state

Obsolete *adj.* no longer useful

oratory *n.* the art of public speaking

orthodoxy *n.* state of conforming to established belief or principle

ostensible *adj.* seemingly, though not actually true or real

ostracism *n.* the exclusion of an individual or group by general consent

Pacification *n.* bringing to a state of peace

pacifist *n.* a person who is opposed to war, and refuses to fight under any circumstances

paean *n.* a song of joy or praise

pagoda *n.* an Asian temple in the form of a pyramidal tower of several stories

panacea *n.* a cure-all

Pandora's box *n.* in Greek mythology, the box sent by the gods to Pandora, which she was forbidden to open. When she opened it out of curiosity, she loosed a swarm of evils upon mankind; a source of much trouble

paradox *n.* something that appears untrue, but may in fact be true

parasitical *adj.* depending on another for support while giving little or nothing in return

pathology *n.* a turning away from an assumed normal state

patrician *n.* a person of breeding and cultivation; aristocrat

patronage *n.* the distribution of government jobs to political supporters

pejoratively *adv.* to refer to something in such a way as to make it seem little or unimportant

penance *n.* an act of self-punishment done for a wrongdoing

peonage *n.* indebted servitude

perestroika *n.* [Russian] restructuring of the economy, government, and society

perjury *n.* lying while under oath

pessimistic *adj.* the attitude of expecting the worst outcome

plebiscite *n.* a popular vote for or against a proposal

pluralism *n.* the existence within a nation of distinct ethnic or other groups

polarized *adj.* divided into two opposing groups

pork barrel *n.* federally financed improvement projects, such as dams, canals, and highways, that are designed to benefit a particular locality

preachment *n.* a long, tiring sermon

precedent *n.* something that occurred earlier that can be cited as a reason for similar action

prerogative *n.* a special right, power, or privilege

prodigious *adj.* of great size and power

profusion *n.* an abundance

prognosticator *n.* one who predicts

proliferation *n.* a rapid increase

propaganda *n.* ideas spread to further one's cause or to damage an opposing cause

prostrate *adj.* laid out flat; helpless

pursuant to *prep.* in agreement with

Quota *n.* a number serving as an upper or lower limit

Radiation *n.* energy emitted as particles or waves

radical *n.* extreme changes or reforms; *adj.* extreme, fundamental

raiments *n.* clothing

rancor *n.* intense ill-will

rationale *n.* the basic reasons for something

rebellion *n.* a struggle against authority or control

recession *n.* a decline in economic activity, less severe and usually shorter than a depression

Reconstruction *n.* the period (1867–1877) during which the former states of the Confederacy were ruled by the federal government or by local Republican governments

referendum *n.* a popular vote to accept or reject a proposal or law

refugee *n.* a person who flees from one country or region to seek refuge in another

regime *n.* a form of government

remunerative *adj.* profitable; rewarding

repression *n.* a strict control which keeps a person or people from behaving naturally

resolution *n.* a formal expression of opinion or intent voted by an official body

rhetoric *n.* the art of writing or speaking persuasively; exaggerated speaking or writing

right wing *adj.* showing conservative tendencies in politics

Salient *adj.* standing out conspicuously

SALT *n.* *Strategic Arms Limitation Treaties:* SALT I, signed in May 1972, and SALT II, signed in June 1979. Both aimed to slow down the nuclear arms race. SALT II was not ratified by the U.S. Senate.

sanction *n.* a penalty used to induce compliance

sanctuary *n.* a place of shelter and protection

satellite nations *n.* nations that are subservient to another nation, especially the nations of Eastern and Central Europe that were dominated by the Soviet Union after World War II

sclerotic *adj.* affected by thickening or hardening of tissue

scourge *n.* a cause of widespread suffering

segregation *n.* separating people according to some standard in schools, housing, industry, and public facilities

selective service *n.* a system by which men are called up for military service; a draft

sensate *adj.* preoccupied with that which can be experienced through the senses

servitude *n.* the obligation to serve a master; bondage; slavery

sexism *n.* discrimination on the basis of sex

Shiite *n.* a member of a major branch of the Islamic faith

social service *n.* the organized assistance of the sick or unfortunate

sociologist *n.* one who studies society, social institutions, and social relationships

sovereign *adj.* controlled by its own authority

speakeasy *n.* an illegal bar during Prohibition

stagnation *n.* a state of not advancing or developing

stalemate *n.* a deadlock

standard of living *n.* a rough measure of the material well-being of a person or group in society

status quo *n.* the way things are at a particular time

stewardship *n.* the duties and obligations of one who oversees an office or estate

subpoena *v.* to serve a legal order requiring someone or something to appear in court for questioning or inspection

subversive *n.* one who attempts to undermine or overthrow an existing government

subvert *v.* to undermine, overthrow, destroy

suffrage *n.* the right to vote

summit *n.* a meeting of the heads of state of two or more countries

sunder *v.* to sever completely or violently

superfluous *adj.* beyond what is necessary

superpower *n.* one of the most militarily powerful nations (in many years since World War II, the US and USSR)

supplant *v.* to take the place of

supplicant *adj.* begging in a humble way

supranational *adj.* going beyond national boundaries, authority, or interests

synthesis *n.* the combination of parts so as to form a whole

synthetic *adj.* artificial

Tactical *adj.* concerning the maneuvering of military forces in battle

tenaciousness *n.* stubbornness; persistence

tenacity *n.* the quality of holding on or retaining strongly

215

tenuous *adj.* not substantial; flimsy

Third Reich *n.* the German state under the Nazis from 1933 to 1945

Third World *n.* nations that profess not to be allied with either the Soviets and their satellite nations or the United States and its allies; especially the developing countries of Asia, Africa, and Latin America

38th parallel *adj.* line of latitude; the location of the dividing line between North and South Korea

totalitarian *adj.* of or relating to a form of rule in which the central government holds absolute control over the lives of its citizens

totalitarianism *n.* the practices and beliefs of a totalitarian government

troubadour *n.* a court poet of the late Middle Ages who wrote poems, often concerning love

Ubiquitous *adj.* being or seeming to be everywhere at the same time

unification *n.* the act of uniting

unilateral *adj.* done by one person or party

utopian *adj.* characterized by impossibly visionary goals

Vanquish *v.* to conquer or defeat in battle

vehicle *n.* a means of transport; anything through which a message is delivered

vigilante *n.* one who, without authority, seeks out and punishes crime

visa *n.* an official permit stamped in a passport allowing entry or travel within a nation

visceral *adj.* instinctive

vogue *n.* fashionable; popular

Welfare state *n.* a social system in which the state assumes responsibility for the welfare of its citizens

Yalta *n.* a Soviet city on the Black Sea (wartime site of a conference in 1945 attended by Franklin D. Roosevelt, Winston Churchill, and Josef Stalin)

Acknowledgments

Interior and Cover Design: Carol Rose **Photo Research:** Sandi Rygiel/Picture Research Consultants **Design Services:** Marc Mgrditchian

Cover: "Dayglow" quilt by Judith Lazelere; **viii,** Culver Pictures, Inc.; **2,** Santi Visalli/The Image Bank; **5,** Historical Pictures Service—Chicago; **6,** Brown Brothers; **9,** Sozio from Fortune Magazine, June 1939; **10,** Birdseye is a registered trademark of Kraft General Foods, Inc. Reproduced with permission; **12,** Jean-Claude Lejeune/Stock Boston; **14,** Bob Daemmrich/Stock Boston; **17,** Leo Castelli Gallery, Bruno Bischofberger Collection/Photo Shunk-Kender; **18,** Victor Hasselblad Inc.; **20, 23,** Brown Brothers; **25,** The John Hay Library, Brown University, photo by Brooke Hammerle; **26,** The Bettmann Archive; **28,** Brown Brothers; **31,** UPI/Bettmann Newsphotos; **32,** Culver Pictures, Inc.; **36,** AP/Wide World Photos; **37,** The Bettmann Archive; **38,** Culver Pictures, Inc.; **40,** UPI/Bettmann Newsphotos; **42,** UPI/Franklin D. Roosevelt Library; **44,** UPI/Bettmann; **47,** E. Irving Blomstrann/The New Britain Museum of American Art; **48,** UPI/Bettmann; **50,** Franklin D. Roosevelt Library; **53, 54,** UPI/Bettmann; **56,** St. Paul Daily News/Minnesota Historical Society; **58,** Franklin D. Roosevelt Library; **60,** John Launois/Black Star; **62, 65,** UPI/Bettmann; **66, 69, 71,** AP/Wide World Photos; **72,** The Bettmann Archive; **75,** UPI/Bettmann Archive; **78,** AP/Wide World Photos; **80,** The Bettmann Archive; **82,** Susan Biddle/The White House; **85, 86,** UPI/Bettmann; **88,** Truman Library; **90,** UPI/Bettmann Archive; **93, 94, 96,** UPI/Bettmann; **99,** Atlan/Sygma; **102,** AP/Wide World Photos; **104, 106,** Bruce Davidson/Magnum Photos; **109,** Eugene Richards/Magnum Photos; **110,** AP/Wide World Photos; **112,** Ralph Crane/Life Magazine © 1970 Time Inc.; **115,** Joseph Schuyler/Stock Boston; **117,** David Shopper/Stock Boston; **118,** UPI/Bettmann; **120,** UPI/Bettmann Newsphotos; **122,** UPI/Bettmann; **124,** UPI/Bettmann Newsphotos; **126,** Dennis Brack/Black Star; **129,** Howard Sochurek Life Magazine © 1955 Time Warner Inc.; **130,** AP/Wide World Photos; **132,** UPI/Bettmann; **133,** Philip Jones Griffiths/Magnum; **135,** Charles Bennay/Black Star; **136,** UPI/Bettmann Newsphotos; **138,** Marc Riboud/Magnum Photos; **140,** Toshio Sakai/UPI/Bettmann; **143,** UPI/Bettmann Newsphotos; **144,** Arthur Grace/Sygma; **147,** Courtesy Schlesinger Library, Radcliffe College; **148,** Stevan Dohanos/Copyright © 1955 Curtis Publishing Co.; **150,** Courtesy The New Yorker Magazine; **151,** UPI/Bettmann; **153,** Michael Hayman/Stock Boston; **154,** Courtesy of Revlon, Inc.; **156,** Jerry Ohlinger; **158,** Liane Enkells/Stock Boston; **161,** Susan McElhinney/Woodfin Camp & Associates; **162, 164, 166,** UPI/Bettmann; **168,** Brown Brothers; **170,** UPI/Bettmann; **172, 174,** AP/Wide World Photos; **177,** Susan Meiselas/Magnum Photos; **178,** Randy Taylor/Gamma-Liaison; **180,** Frank LaBua/Liaison International; **183,** Alex Webb/Magnum Photos; **184,** Eric Sander/Gamma-Liaison; **187,** UPI/Bettmann; **188,** J.P. Laffont/Sygma; **190, 193,** Reuters/Bettmann Newsphotos; **195,** AP/Wide World Photos; **197,** P.D. Driscoll/Gamma-Liaison; **198,** Courtesy of McDonald's Restaurants of Canada—Limited; **200, 203,** AP/Wide World Photos; **205,** Bill Swersey/Gamma-Liaison; **206,** Patrick Piel/Gamma-Liaison; **208,** AP/Wide World Photos.